KT-567-392

Poverty and Social Exclusion in Europe

Matt Barnes
Research Fellow, University of Bath, UK

Christopher Heady
Professor of Applied Economics, University of Bath, UK

Sue Middleton
Senior Research Fellow and Co-Director of the Centre for Research in Social Policy, Loughborough University, UK

Jane Millar
Professor of Social Policy and Director of the Centre for the Analysis of Social Policy, University of Bath, UK

Fotis Papadopoulos
Researcher, Athens University of Economics and Business, Greece

Graham Room
Professor of European Social Policy, University of Bath, UK

Panos Tsakloglou
Associate Professor, Department of International and European Economic Studies, Athens University of Economics and Business, Greece

Edward Elgar
Cheltenham, UK • Northampton, MA, USA

© Matt Barnes, Christopher Heady, Sue Middleton, Jane Millar, Fotis Papadopoulos, Graham Room, Panos Tsakloglou, 2002

All rights reserved. No part of this publication may be reproduced, stored in a retrieval system or transmitted in any form or by any means, electronic, mechanical or photocopying, recording, or otherwise without the prior permission of the publisher.

Published by
Edward Elgar Publishing Limited
Glensanda House
Montpellier Parade
Cheltenham
Glos GL50 1UA
UK

Edward Elgar Publishing, Inc.
136 West Street
Suite 202
Northampton
Massachusetts 01060
USA

A catalogue record for this book
is available from the British Library

Library of Congress Cataloguing in Publication Data

Poverty and social exclusion in Europe / Matt Barnes . . . [et al.].
    p. cm.
  Includes index.
    1. Marginality, Social—Europe.   2. Poverty—Europe.   3. Public welfare—Europe.   4. Socially handicapped—Europe.   5. Europe—Social policy.   6. Europe—Economic policy.   I. Barnes, Matt.
  HN376.P68   2002
  305.5'6'094—dc21   2001040771

ISBN 1 84064 375 7 (cased)

Printed and bound in Great Britain by Biddles Ltd, *www.biddles.co.uk*

Contents

Figures

Tables

Acknowledgements

The material for this book is drawn from the work of an international group of researchers involved in a three-year project funded by the European Union under its Targeted Socio-economic Research Programme. The authors are grateful for the support of the European Commission and Eurostat in assisting us with the project.

The authors also wish to thank in particular our partners in the project who provided, amongst other things, policy papers about the four risk groups in their countries. In addition to the project co-ordinators, the leaders of these teams of researchers were Christoph Badelt, Abteilung Sozialpolitik, Institut fuer Volkswirtschaftstheorie und Politik, Vienna, Austria; Wolfgang Vosges, Zentrum fur Sozialpolitik, Bremen, Germany; Ivar Lødemel, Institute for Applied Social Science (FAFO), Oslo, Norway; Isabel Baptista, Centro de Estudos para a Intervencão Social, (CESIS) Lisbon, Portugal. Many other researchers, too numerous to mention, have taken part in the project at various points and we are grateful for their contribution.

Finally, grateful thanks to Angela Waite and Julie Birch in the Centre for Research in Social Policy who prepared the manuscript for publication.

Introduction

Jane Millar and Sue Middleton

There are estimated to be almost 60 million people across the European Union living in poverty, defined as having incomes below half the average for their country. Poverty rates vary from country to country, as do the types of families and households most at risk of poverty, and the circumstances in which poor people live. This raises many questions about the ways in which markets, families and state provisions combine in various ways to produce distinct welfare outcomes in different countries.

Our capacity to analyse and understand the nature and causes of these cross-national variations has been greatly enhanced in recent years by related theoretical and methodological developments. On the theoretical side, the increasing interest in 'social exclusion' has focused attention away from narrow income-based definitions of poverty to much broader and multi-dimensional definitions of economic and social disadvantage, and to the processes by which these are linked in place and time. There has also been an increased interest in the dynamics of poverty and social exclusion and how individuals and families change their status over time. This has involved both longitudinal studies, following the same people over time, and life-course analysis, focusing on what happens to people as they face particular 'risk' situations, such as illness or divorce.

Methodologically, the creation of large data sets that provide detailed social and economic information on individuals and households over periods of several years has made multi-dimensional, dynamic and life-course analyses much more feasible in practice. The European Community Household Panel (ECHP) is one such data set that provides a new opportunity to examine the extent, nature and impact of social exclusion in Europe. It collects information on a range of social and economic factors, following the same people over time. It also has the unique advantage of being genuinely comparative across countries – the same questions are asked in all the participating countries, at the same time, and the same socio-economic measures can be constructed. It thus provides the first opportunity for an empirically based cross-national comparison of both the multi-dimensional nature of social exclusion, and the dynamic processes of social exclusion and inclusion.

This book reports on analysis of the second wave of the ECHP survey, originally carried out under the EU programme of Targeted Socio-Economic Research, as part of a three-year project bringing together multi-disciplinary research teams in Austria, Germany, Greece, Norway, Portugal and the UK. The project was co-ordinated from Greece and the UK and the book has been written by the research co-ordinators. The policy descriptions and analysis are based on papers provided by our partners in each of the six countries whose contribution to this volume is gratefully acknowledged.

The main aims of the study were to explore the nature and processes of social exclusion in six European countries in the mid to late 1990s through multi-dimensional, life-course and dynamic analyses and to relate the findings to the different policy environments in each country.

The countries were chosen to reflect different configurations of public and private welfare so that comparisons could be made of the impact of government policy on levels and durations of poverty and social exclusion. Austria, Germany, Greece, Norway, Portugal and the United Kingdom (UK) include at least one representative of each of the three welfare regimes identified by Esping-Andersen's seminal, if controversial, typology (Esping- Andersen, 1990). Austria and Germany represent the conservative 'corporatist' tradition said to be characterised by status-preserving inter-vention which encourages family and motherhood, discourages women from working and preserves the model of the one (male) breadwinner family supported by benefits and taxation. Norway is a member of the Nordic group of countries typified by 'social-democratic' welfare systems in which individuals are favoured over families and social policies are uni-versal, providing high levels of benefits and services, funded by relatively high levels of taxation[1]. The United Kingdom represents the 'liberal' strand of Esping-Andersen's typology. State provision is limited, providing low flat-rate and means-tested benefits, and individuals are encouraged, by incentives and by default, to make their own provision through the market. Finally, Greece and Portugal are said to be representatives of a fourth type – the rudimentary welfare states – characterised by minimal welfare poli-cies, reliance on family solidarity, a large informal sector and a recent history of authoritarian politics.

Of course no country fits neatly into any one of these four welfare types and, as we will show, these six countries are no exception. In any event, it is our view that the categorising of countries according to welfare struc-tures may not be the best method of exploring poverty and social exclusion. Most of these structures grew piecemeal. They were designed on the basis of traditional views of gender roles – male breadwinner, female carer – at a time when individuals' lives tended to be static geographically, relationally and economically. All these aspects of life in a (post-)modern society are characterised by rapid change. The inheritance of static policies and institutions is ill-suited to meet the demands of the 'new modernity', characterised by dynamism, individualism and diversity in lifestyles and living standards. Comparative analysis focusing on the outcomes of welfare delivery systems for groups of the population experiencing change, rather than on the delivery systems themselves, may provide better guidance as to if and how such systems need to be reformed and restructured to meet the needs of life in twenty-first century Europe.

This book will focus on two main aspects of the study. First it will examine the nature and extent of multi-dimensional disadvantage in the six different national contexts. Second it will focus on four life-course 'risk groups' – young adulthood, lone parenthood, long-term sickness and retirement – in order to compare the outcomes of these risk situations for families and households across the six countries. The analysis here is cross-sectional and explores in detail the nature of multi-dimensional disadvantage in different countries at times of change in the life course. A companion volume (to be published later in 2002) will focus on the dynamic analysis.

In Chapter 1, Matt Barnes explains the purpose and rationale of this research and places it in the context of other recent studies. This chapter also describes the ECHP and the main definitions used in the analysis. Chapter 2, by Panos Tsakloglou and Fotis Papadopoulos, examines the methodology required to investigate the extent, depth and degree of social exclusion using the ECHP survey and presents an analysis of the relationship between low incomes and different dimensions of social exclusion. Chapters 3–6 – by Sue Middleton, Jane Millar and Chris Heady – look in detail at the four risk groups – young adults, lone parents, sick and disabled people, and retired people. In the final chapter, Chris Heady and Graham Room draw out policy implications.

NOTE

1. Norway is not a member of the EU and does not participate in the ECHP. The results for Norway are from the Norwegian Living Standards Survey that includes similar questions to those asked in the ECHP. This means that some of the tables do not include Norway, if comparable data were not available.

1. Social exclusion and the life course

Matt Barnes

INTRODUCTION

> The poor shall be taken to mean persons, families and groups of persons where
> resources (material, cultural and social) are so limited as to exclude them from
> a minimum acceptable way of life in the Member States in which they live.
> (European Commission, 1984)

This book focuses on poverty, multi-dimensional disadvantage, social
exclusion and the life course in six European countries: Austria, Germany,
Greece, Norway, Portugal and the United Kingdom. It is based on a
European Union (EU) funded project: 'Family formation, labour market
participation and the dynamics of social exclusion'.[1] The main purpose of
the book is to investigate indicators of poverty and social exclusion for four
risk groups of individuals who might be at particular risk of experiencing
these states – young adults, lone parents, sick or disabled people and retired
people. A common understanding of terms associated with poverty, multi-
dimensional disadvantage and social exclusion are established, in both
policy discussions and policy implementation, in the context of the 'risk
group' individuals and the country in which they live.

The book has three main objectives:

1. to increase the understanding of poverty and multi-dimensional disad-
    vantage in Europe and to identify indicators of social exclusion;
2. to examine and compare the extent and impact of poverty and multi-
    dimensional disadvantage among individuals in four high risk groups
    – young adults, lone parents, sick or disabled people and retired people
    and
3. to establish the ways in which the policies of Member States affect the
    risk of poverty, multi-dimensional disadvantage and social exclusion
    for individuals in these groups.

Poverty is measured using traditional methods associated with the distribution of household incomes, whilst dimensions of disadvantage measured

include the possession of household items, housing quality, labour market status, health and social participation. In an attempt to understand the underlying nature of multi-dimensional disadvantage, the book looks at the correlation between different dimensions of deprivation, and examines the relevance of using alternative measures of household resources other than income.

Few of the countries under investigation have explicit studies of multi-dimensional disadvantage. Some of the countries have a long tradition of empirical research on issues of poverty and low living standards; this is the case, especially for the UK and, to a lesser extent, Germany. The remaining countries have less research history, with such studies only beginning to appear since the 1980s. By examining poverty and multi-dimensional disadvantage in these six European countries, useful concepts and indicators can be defined both at a national and European level.

The project is based on an analysis of the European Community Household Panel (ECHP) and for Norway from the Norwegian Living Standards Survey. The recent establishment of the ECHP means data on multi-dimensional disadvantage is available on a consistent basis for all EU countries for the first time. The ECHP contains detailed information on income, non-monetary deprivation indicators, labour market status and social participation, as well as socio-economic characteristics of the household.

The analysis of the relationship between the empirical results and public policy will be conducted for each country individually, which is particularly useful for those with limited studies in the area, and, more importantly, at a comparative level. Thus, comparisons will be made between countries of the extent to which multi-dimensional disadvantage can arise at certain stages of the life course. The relation of these comparisons to the policy differences between countries, and the differences in family responsibilities, will provide fresh insights into how policy measures to reduce and eradicate social exclusion can be improved.

Although poverty and social exclusion, and the role of the welfare state in alleviating these, are currently at the centre of the public discourse in all countries under examination, on the whole there remains little use of multi-dimensional disadvantage for the design of policies to relieve these problems. Identifying different aspects of multi-dimensional disadvantage is important in assessing whether policies to combat social exclusion and promote re-integration should be formulated as a series of independent programmes focused on particular aspects of deprivation, or as a single comprehensive policy. The book will explore this multi-dimensional approach, where appropriate, by analysing the consequences of different mixes of public and private support to people who are deprived or are at risk of becoming socially excluded.

The countries covered in the book come from a range of welfare regime typologies including Norway, where public support seems to have almost eradicated poverty; Greece and Portugal, where public support plays a much smaller role than families and non-state organisations and where poverty rates remain high; and the UK, Austria and Germany, countries with well developed welfare states but continuing problems of poverty.

POVERTY, MULTI-DIMENSIONAL DISADVANTAGE AND SOCIAL EXCLUSION

Poverty and Multi-Dimensional Disadvantage

Poverty has long been a contested notion. Traditionally, the intellectual understanding of poverty has focused upon distributional issues: the lack of resources at the disposal of an individual or household – primarily the lack of income. Rowntree (1901) defined an absolute measure of poverty; a level of income designed to provide a minimum standard of living based on a person's biological needs for food, water, clothing and shelter. 'My primary poverty line represented the minimum sum on which physical efficiency could be maintained. It was a bare standard of subsistence rather than living' (Rowntree, 1941).

Absolute definitions of poverty are criticised for a number of reasons. First, it is generally agreed that it is very difficult to define 'the minimum on which physical efficiency can be maintained'. Not only is it problematic to determine what is meant by a minimum physical efficiency, it is also difficult to equate this with a sum of money from which this can be achieved. Secondly, even if this was possible, standards of living change between individuals, cultures, societies and, importantly, over time. Thirdly, an absolute definition determines sufficient resources at the level of physical needs and not on broader social and cultural needs.

During the 1960s, various experts worked on developing a more sophisticated approach to the definition of poverty. Peter Townsend's definitive work on poverty in the United Kingdom (Townsend, 1979) went beyond an absolute definition based on physical needs, to view poverty in relation to a generally accepted standard of living, in a specific society, at a particular time.

> Individuals . . . can be said to be in poverty when they lack the resources to obtain the types of diet, participate in the activities and have the living conditions and amenities which are customary, or at least widely encouraged or approved, in the societies to which they belong. (Townsend, 1979, p. 31.)

This definition focuses on the distribution of resources, not just income, and the level of resources that individuals need to participate in ordinary living patterns, customs and activities. Townsend defined an income poverty line to reflect the point at which individuals are unable to participate fully in the life of the society in which they live. Townsend's work became the foundation on which much of contemporary poverty debates were built.

As with the seminal work of Rowntree, Townsend's approach received various criticisms. Sen (1983) criticised Townsend's purely relativist notions of poverty, arguing that there is 'an irreducible absolutist core in the idea of poverty'. Sen argued that in certain cases, for example starvation or hunger, the relative picture has to take a back seat behind the possibly dominating absolutist consideration. In other words, if there is starvation or hunger, then no matter what the relative picture looks like, there clearly is poverty (for further information see the debate between Sen and Townsend in *Oxford Economic Papers*: Townsend, 1985 and Sen, 1985).

Other authors criticised Townsend's attempt to define a society's customary resources and participation activities. Much debate focused on how to take into account what resources and participation activities people choose to manage without (Piachaud, 1981).

Ringen (1985, 1988) has argued that there is a theoretical inconsistency with using an indirect measure of resources – income – to measure a direct concept of deprivation. To understand the notion of poverty it is necessary to focus on a range of resources, not simply income, so that using an income poverty line to summarise such deprivation is conceptually and empirically flawed. Research has shown that the relationship between income and deprivation is rather looser than would be expected *a priori* (Mack and Lansley, 1985; Callan et al., 1993). There are substantial proportions of households with relatively large incomes that are lacking in terms of non-monetary indicators of deprivation. And, in the other direction, a majority of those in low income groups do not suffer from deprivation, as measured by absence of particular items because of lack of resources (Nolan et al., 1999).

This work has led to a general consensus about the nature of poverty and the most suitable method of measuring the phenomenon. Poverty is not simply about income, but about a lack of resources that impedes participation in society. Measuring poverty requires more than simply information on income. It requires detailed analysis of the relationship between income and other resources, concentrating on measures of multiple deprivation and on participation issues. Income is a major factor in the understanding of poverty, but one that should be used as a starting point for broadening the analysis into issues of multi-dimensional disadvantage.

'Social Exclusion'

The latest development in the debate about poverty and disadvantage is the use of the term 'social exclusion'. Social exclusion has become a 'buzz' word in political discourse, particularly that of the European Commission, but also of a selection of EU national governments. The term first appeared in French literature in the 1970s. Origins of the term derive from the idea of society as a status hierarchy comprising people bound together by rights and obligations that reflect, and are defined with respect to, a shared moral order. Those excluded from this moral order often experienced marginalisation in terms of employment and their relationship with the state (Lee and Murie, 1999).

Graham Room has been influential in the conceptualisation and measurement of social exclusion at a European level. Room hosted a seminar on social exclusion at the University of Bath in 1994, where he recommended that Eurostat should change from a financial concept of poverty to a multi-dimensional concept. He provides an analysis of whether and how social exclusion differs from poverty (Room, 1999). He argues that much of what is claimed as new in the analysis of social exclusion can also be found in poverty studies. Nevertheless the added value from the concept of social exclusion comes from the way these different elements are combined. He points to five key factors:

1. social exclusion is multi-dimensional – not about income alone but a wide range of indicators of living standards;
2. social exclusion is dynamic – analysing social exclusion means understanding a process and identifying the factors which can trigger entry or exit;
3. social exclusion has a neighbourhood dimension – deprivation is caused not only by lack of personal resources but also by insufficient or unsatisfactory community facilities, such as run-down schools, remotely-sited shops, poor public transport networks and so on;
4. social exclusion is relational – the notion of poverty is primarily focused upon distributional issues, the lack of resources at the disposal of an individual or a household. In contrast, social exclusion focuses more on relational issues: in other words, inadequate social participation, lack of social integration and lack of power; and
5. social exclusion implies a major discontinuity in relationships with the rest of society.

The notion of social exclusion has the potential not just to highlight differences in resources between individuals and groups of individuals, but also to explore the key issues of autonomy and dependency. Likewise the relational analysis points to the importance of placing the individual in context, and understanding the constraints and opportunities that they face, including the way in which their personal responsibilities and obligations affect their capacity to be self-supporting, and to support others (Millar, 2001).

As Williams and Pillinger (1996, p. 9) state, whereas 'poverty studies have concentrated on a lack of access to material resources, the concept of social exclusion provides a framework to look at the social relations of power and control, the processes of marginalisation and exclusion, and the complex and multi-faceted ways in which these operate'. Such social and cultural injustices are seen to be generated by inequalities of gender, race, ethnicity, sexuality, age and disability.

However, just as there was no clear and agreed distinction between the various theories of poverty, so the notion of social exclusion can mean many different things and be underpinned by very different values systems. For example, Levitas (1998) distinguishes between underclass, redistributive and integrative discourses of social exclusion. Most authors, though, have tried to distinguish between poverty and social exclusion by pointing to the wider meaning of the latter concept. For example, Tony Atkinson (1998) argues that social exclusion has three main elements: relativity (it implies exclusion from a particular society at a particular time and place); agency (it implies an act or acts, by an agent or agents); and dynamics (people are excluded not just because of their current situation, but also because they have little prospect for the future). According to his viewpoint, it is perhaps the agency and dynamic aspects of social exclusion that distinguish it from an understanding of multi-dimensional disadvantage proposed by authors such as Townsend and Ringen.

A prominent author in the operationalisation of the notion of social exclusion is the French sociologist Paugam. He has concentrated his work on the relational aspect of social exclusion, especially in respect to occupational relationships and family support experienced by unemployed people in France. His study revealed that despite experiencing a transition into unemployment, men in his study were unable to draw on support from family members, and in fact saw these relationships erode (Paugam, 1995). It was a slightly different story for women who were able to maintain their family links to a much greater extent. In another piece of work (Paugam, 1996), he shows that the French experience is reflected in some other large urban-industrial societies of Northern Europe. This is in contrast to the experience of some Southern European countries, where the extended family seems to play a much stronger role.

Within the countries represented in this book, widely differing definitions of social exclusion exist. German authors tend to view social exclusion in the same way as they view long-term poverty. In Portugal authors have made distinctions between low living standards and exclusion. In Norway social exclusion is used to denote marginalisation (that is deprivation in both material and social terms) (Tsakloglou, 1998).

Conceptualisation

Given the range of theories on poverty, multi-dimensional disadvantage and social exclusion that abound in the literature, it is necessary to clarify where the focus of this book lies. Conceptualising poverty, multi-dimensional disadvantage and social exclusion can help to clarify policy goals. For example policies aimed at tackling disadvantage, and in particular social exclusion, should use a much wider range of tools than poverty alleviation methods that focus primarily on raising income levels at a point in time. One way to simplify the differences between the concepts is to categorise the main features of each approach.

Such a categorisation as that presented in Table 1.1 is, of course, open to

Table 1.1 Conceptualisation and measurement – poverty, deprivation and social exclusion

	Poverty	Deprivation	Social exclusion
Concept	Uni-dimensional	Multi-dimensional	Multi-dimensional
	Physical needs	Physical needs, Relative material needs	Physical needs, relative material needs, societal participation
	Distributional	Distributional	Distributional, Relational
	Static	Static	Dynamic
Measurement	Indirect	Direct	Direct
	Outcome indicator	Outcome indicators	Outcome indicators, Process indicators, risk factors
	Income resources	Income resources, non-monetary resources	Income resources, non-monetary resources, capability to participate
	Individual, household	Individual, household	Individual, household, community

criticism. In reality, many of the distinctions between the concepts, and ways of measuring them, merge together. However, the table is useful because it clarifies the focus of this study as closer to a notion of multi-dimensional disadvantage rather than to poverty or social exclusion. Our analysis is quite clearly moving away from the type of investigation that concentrates only on income distributions and poverty lines (although this is still an integral part of the analysis) to a more multi-dimensional definition of disadvantage. Although the book focuses on the materially poor, there is some examination of indicators of social participation.

This analysis is not looking at the dynamic processes involved in moves into and out of social exclusion, but at indicators of disadvantage for individuals at a single point in time. These indicators may well imply that groups of individuals are at risk of social exclusion and indeed will provide estimates of the numbers who are experiencing varying degrees of multi-dimensional disadvantage. However, the indicators are unable to capture all the features of social exclusion that the notion represents – for example whether individuals are moving towards or away from multi-dimensional disadvantage, or the effect of community facilities on an individual's standard of living.

Using a notion of multi-dimensional disadvantage, we employ alternative definitions of resources to examine the composition of the 'materially poor', although also investigating social relations, and the extent to which the alternative criteria identify the same segments of the population as poor. There are two components here: the analysis of the correlation between different aspects of multi-dimensional disadvantage, and the analysis of the relevance of different measures of deprivation. Thus analysis will provide an idea of which are the better indicators of deprivation for use in policies to combat multi-dimensional disadvantage and social exclusion.

The European Community Household Panel survey is used to measure the correlations between indicators across households. This will involve answering questions such as: to what extent is the presence of one aspect of disadvantage associated with the presence of other aspects? In addition to the descriptive aspect, the project will look at explanations of these patterns. Can they be explained in terms of the broader range of resources available to individuals and households, enabling them differentially to take advantage of new opportunities or to survive new adversities? These resources include, of course, the resources provided through the social security and education systems. But they also include the resources offered by members of the extended family, the local community and the employer.

Cross-national, or comparative, studies of multi-dimensional disadvantage can take these investigations further. Cross-national comparison opens the way to exploring how different policy assumptions translate into different standards of living for different groups of individuals. Such analysis is central to unpacking the indicators and potential causes of multi-dimensional disadvantage and social exclusion in different types of welfare state. Cross-national comparisons allow investigation of how far these causes are true for other countries, investigating further findings such as those that suggest there are indeed significant differences in poverty and multi-dimensional disadvantage outcomes for groups of individuals living in different types of policy regime.

FOUR DIFFERENT LIFE STAGES – GROUPS AT 'RISK' OF SOCIAL EXCLUSION

Life-Course Analysis

The importance of demographic factors, including such standard events as young adults leaving home, marriage, divorce and retirement, has led to the development of 'life-course analysis' (see Walker and Ashworth, 1994) as an approach to understanding poverty. This approach identifies particular stages of life at which the risks of poverty are especially high. By concentrating on young adults, lone parents, sick or disabled people, and retired people, the book is focusing on the risks of social exclusion that arise at particularly significant stages of the life course.

Two of the life-stage groups, young adults and retired people, represent universal stages of the life course. For young adults, leaving the parental home, entering the labour market for the first time or continuing into further education, can make the individual at risk of disadvantage or exclusion. Similarly for retired people, leaving the labour market in particular can make the individual, and the household, vulnerable to disadvantage and exclusion.

The other two groups of interest in the project, lone parents and sick or disabled people, represent life circumstances that not all individuals will experience. Being a lone parent, or being sick or disabled, are states that individuals may be in for varying length of times, entering or leaving according to different life events. Such events associated with these groups – giving birth, separating from a partner, forced withdrawal from the labour market, reliance on social transfers, loss of mobility – may also lead to a reduction in living standards and changes in lifestyles.

Constructing the 'Risk Groups'

Choosing the exact definition of the 'risk groups' to be examined is crucial to an understanding of multi-dimensional disadvantage for these groups of individuals. The risk group definitions must be able to select individuals who share common circumstances and experiences related to their life-stage. The risk groups also need to be identified across countries to enable national material to be comparable. The risk group definitions are presented in Table 1.2.

Table 1.2   Risk group definitions

Risk group	Definition
Young adults	Individuals between 16 and 29 years of age.
Lone parents	Individuals over 16 years of age and below state retirement age: 1. who live without a cohabiting partner but with at least one dependent child (under 16 years or in full-time education). 2. who live without a cohabiting partner but with children – all of whom are non-dependent.
Sick or disabled people	Individuals over 16 years of age and below state retirement age: whose health in general is very bad, or who are hampered severely in daily activities.
Retired people	1. adults over 45 years of age who declare themselves as retired. 2. adults who do not declare themselves as retired but who are over state retirement age and not working full-time (16 or more hours per week).

The young adulthood risk group is the most straightforward to construct, as it only uses the age of the individual as a defining parameter. However, amongst individuals in this age group are various sub-groups that require separate investigation, especially those at particular risk of social exclusion. These groups include young adults still in education, those who have left the parental home and those out of the labour market.

The definition of lone parents is designed to account for the fact that lone-parent households can vary quite considerably both within and between countries. Within countries the situation of lone-parent households who have to rely solely on the lone parent for income can be very different from those who have other 'breadwinners' in the household. From a comparative perspective family structure varies quite considerably between the prolonged, supportive southern European households and the more short-term, independent northern European households. By distinguishing between lone-parent families with and without dependent children, the book allows analysis to focus on the typical lone-parent type in each country, as well as making comparisons with alternative family types.

The definition of sickness or disability used in the book is based on subjective assessments of individuals' health. The definition is relatively strict, choosing those who believe their health to be very bad (the fifth point of a five-point scale) or who feel hampered severely in their daily activities. The sickness or disability risk group is limited to adults below state retirement age. Finally, the definition of retirement – those over 45 years of age who say they are retired and those over state retirement age who are not working full-time even if they do not say that they are retired – includes a subjective and objective element. The subjective element captures all those who say they are retired, including early retirees. The objective element captures those over state retirement age who are not working full-time, whether they state they are retired or not. This is intended to pick up those who are of retirement status but do not describe themselves as retired, most often women.

Although the four life stages differ in many respects, the analysis in each case seeks to elucidate the immediate and medium-term outcomes of each, and the particular combination of circumstances that cause some people to experience multi-dimensional disadvantage. Specialised surveys that concentrate on and cover vulnerable population groups provide a detailed account of the living standards of these groups. However these surveys often miss the wider picture of living standards in the population as a whole. The book includes detailed analysis of our chosen vulnerable risk groups and provides comparisons with larger populations, not only within countries but across countries. This allows an examination of other factors, such as unemployment or welfare provisions, in the context of the experience of the life-stage individuals both within and across countries.

Risk Groups and Social Policy

Social policy systems work with, and often help to shape, the different phases and stages of an individual's life course. For each of the four life stages, policy analysis investigates various aspects of the problems of multi-dimensional disadvantage and social exclusion that can arise. These include the perceived size of the problem, the effectiveness of existing policies, related policy debates and institutional frameworks already in place to deal with the problem (for a discussion of policy making and the life course, see Leisering and Walker, 1998).

This study addresses key issues in relation to each of the four risk groups. For young adults, the research focuses on the experience of young people between the ages of 16 and 29 years. Particular considerations include young adults' experiences of education and work, unemployment and training; lifestyles after leaving home; the nature of the accommodation attained by young adults; and the financial and social circumstances of the home.

For lone parents, attention concentrates on the experience of lone parenthood: the circumstances of men and women in lone parenthood; the experiences during lone parenthood including financial support and the flexibility of employment options.

For the retired, issues to be addressed include: the level of post retirement incomes; the balance between different forms of financial support; lifestyles and social relations in retirement; and the relationship between retirement, early retirement and health. For sick or disabled people, the analysis investigates how households manage if one of their members is ill and whether current social provision is sufficient to reduce the risk of social exclusion.

POVERTY, MULTI-DIMENSIONAL DISADVANTAGE AND SOCIAL EXCLUSION IN EUROPE: EVIDENCE FROM RECENT RESEARCH

European Poverty Research

At this point it is useful to review the history of European research, particularly at EU level, on poverty, multi-dimensional disadvantage and social exclusion. This provides background and context to our study – not only in relation to empirical findings and policy analysis, but also in terms of methodological advances and changes in political discourse.

The growth of poverty has been the concern of European policy makers since poverty work at the European level began to get off the ground in the mid-1970s. The first European anti-poverty programme ran from 1975 to 1980, including nine national reports on poverty and anti-poverty policy. The second anti-poverty programme (1986–89) contained no research element, instead concentrating on national policies to eradicate the phenomenon. The third programme (1990–94) saw the reinstatement of a series of cross-national studies (see O'Higgins and Jenkins, 1990; ISSAS, 1990; Hagenaars et al., 1994).

In the early years of European-level poverty research, one of the problems of conducting studies was the lack of comparable, quality poverty data. During the second anti-poverty programme the statistical office of the European Commission, Eurostat, was engaged to work on the long-term improvement of poverty indicators. Part of this work involved discussions between Eurostat and national statistical offices concerning the use of household budget surveys for producing comparable data on low-income groups (Room, 1995a).

Until the third anti-poverty programme, studies centred around poor populations, based on an analysis of income or expenditure distributions, and poverty lines. The third programme made considerable progress in the use of different poverty concepts and measures and the ranking of countries according to these (Ramprakash, 1994). Using data from national household surveys, Eurostat drew poverty lines at 40, 50 and 60 per cent of the national average equivalent expenditure, ranking countries according to the proportion of the population in poverty. Low rates of poverty were found in Belgium, the Netherlands and Luxembourg (between 2 and 5 per cent). Countries with the highest poverty rates included Portugal, Italy and Greece (between 11 and 16 per cent).

The research suggested that similar groups of individuals were the most likely to experience poverty across virtually all Member States. These groups included households headed by unemployed persons, retired persons and those 'looking after the home'; single elderly and large households; households in which nobody was working; female-headed households; households headed by an elderly person; households with heads with low levels of education and households living in certain regions. In a number of countries farmers and agricultural workers also had a high poverty percentage, and the same was true for households living in rural areas and for single-parent households.

These studies were among the first comparative studies to draw on micro-data in Europe. Consequently the research suffered from some serious limitations. One of the main limitations was that the information drawn from each country was still not truly comparable. Not only did some of the national household surveys suffer from small sample sizes, but the survey methodology varied between countries. This meant that attempts to harmonise the information in the surveys proved difficult.

The third anti-poverty programme was also concerned with non-monetary indicators of poverty. The programme was interested in collecting data on the extent to which households possessed certain commodities, could engage in certain activities, or were subjected to financial pressures of various kinds. Work was conducted to assess the usefulness and feasibility of utilising such indicators. Recommendations were made to national statistical organisations to produce relevant, up-to-date and reliable data to allow Eurostat to produce statistics that were as comparable as possible.

Probably the best resourced comparative data on living standards has been that of the Luxembourg Income Study (LIS). The LIS was set up in 1983, gathering together datasets on household income from more than 25 countries, for one or more years. However, work using this source has tended to focus mainly on comparisons of poverty and income inequality, rather than on multi-dimensional disadvantage (for example, Bradbury and Markus, 2001, and Forssén 1998).

More recently, cross-national studies have appeared which are based on national panel surveys. Much of the work on panel surveys developed from the pioneering work of the Panel Study of Income Dynamics, launched at the University of Michigan in 1968 (for example Bane and Ellwood, 1986). Household panel surveys have been set up in various EU countries, but there are few that have been collecting data for a substantial period of time. The Panel Comparability Project (Schaber et al., 1993) has created an international database integrating microdata from various national household panel surveys over a number of years. The database contains consistent, harmonised variables across identical data structures for each country included. Countries covered in the database include Germany, Great Britain, France, Luxembourg and Poland. It is important to stress that in all these databases, the various concepts are harmonised ex post to the extent possible (whereas in the case of the ECHP this harmonisation is done ex ante).

In 1994 Eurostat provided a breakthrough in attempts to provide comparable European poverty and deprivation statistics with the introduction of the European Community Household Panel (ECHP) survey. The survey provided for the first time truly comparable microdata on poverty and deprivation in participating countries of the European Union. Initially the ECHP microdata was only available to researchers inside the European Commission and those employed on European Commission funded projects.[2] Therefore, to date only a few studies have examined income poverty rates across European countries using comparable data and methodologies, let alone information on multi-dimensional disadvantage and social exclusion (one of the few studies to examine social exclusion in relation to the experience of unemployment is Gallie and Paugam, 2000).

Much of the work using the ECHP has indeed focused on income poverty across Europe. This work has mainly been conducted by Eurostat researchers (Eurostat, 1990, 1994). According to Eurostat (1997), 57 million individuals lived in poor households in the EU 12 in 1993. Among them children (less than 16 years of age) accounted for 13 million. The proportion of individuals living in households below the poverty line ranged from 6 per cent in Denmark to 26 per cent in Portugal (see Table 1.3). Eurostat identified certain types of household that were more likely to be poor than others. Households particularly likely to be poor were those that contained a single parent, where all children were under 16 years of age, and where the reference person was unemployed.

Table 1.3 *Proportions below the poverty line in 12 EU countries in 1993, ECHP, wave 1*

	Proportion below the poverty line		
Country	Households	Individuals	Children
EU 12	17	17	20
Denmark	9	6	5
Germany	13	11	13
Belgium	13	13	15
Netherlands	14	13	16
Luxembourg	14	15	23
France	16	14	12
Italy	18	20	24
Spain	19	20	25
Ireland	21	21	28
United Kingdom	23	22	32
Greece	24	22	19
Portugal	29	26	27

Note: Poverty line drawn at 50 per cent of country specific mean equivalised household income.

Source: Eurostat (1997).

Eurostat performed a modest amount of analysis on non-monetary deprivation across the EU 12 countries as a whole. They concluded that income-poor households were more likely to be deprived on a range of non-monetary indicators. However, the analysis only made brief comparisons between countries, and concentrated on a multi-dimensional nature of economic deprivation rather than social exclusion (Eurostat, 2000).

From Poverty to Social Exclusion

The term 'social exclusion' is treated explicitly in a political legal context within the EU, and Article 136 of the Amsterdam Treaty lists 'the combating of exclusion' as one of the six objectives of European social policy (Mejer, 1999). However, at present there are few studies that measure multi-dimensional disadvantage or social exclusion at a European level. Goodin et al. (1999) used panel studies from three countries (Germany, the Netherlands and the United States), to assess the effects of three welfare state typologies on poverty, equality and income distribution, but did not look into broader notions of disadvantage. Some studies have looked at various dimensions of poverty and disadvantage, particularly from a national context, but there is a lack of truly comparable work on the nature of multi-dimensional disadvantage and social exclusion in Europe.

On a national level there have been various attempts to utilise information on the social and economic context in which income-poor people live, assessing the consequences of policies which deal with social protection, education, health and other welfare issues. Such studies have taken place in different countries to a varying degree.

In the UK there has been much recent research and policy interest in the concept of social exclusion. The election of 'New' Labour as the British Government in 1997 saw the acceptance of social exclusion into Government policy discourse. Later the Government's launch of the Social Exclusion Unit provided the opportunity to develop and implement a set of radical and innovative policies to tackle social exclusion. In September 1999 the British Government produced long awaited plans for dealing with poverty and social exclusion in the form of its 'Poverty Audit' White Paper (DSS, 1999a). The report set out the Government's list of priorities for improvements over the coming years, detailing a set of key indicators of poverty and social exclusion. The indicators fall into three broad categories: indicators of poverty, including non-monetary items; indicators of integration, through routes such as work and access to services; and indicators of precipitating factors, such as levels of teenage pregnancy and fear of crime (Lessof and Jowell, 1999).

From a more research-based perspective, the Centre for the Analysis of Social Exclusion at the London School of Economics has sought to operationalise social exclusion by means of five dimensions of participation (consumption, savings, production, political and social). These dimensions of participation are used to identify the 'normal activities of citizens in that society' (Burchardt et al., 1999). Analysing British Household Panel Study data from 1991 to 1995, the authors found evidence of a strong association between the five dimensions of 'participation'. However, they found few individuals who were 'excluded' on all dimensions in any one year, and even fewer who had experienced multiple exclusion over the whole period.

Work in other countries on aspects of multi-dimensional disadvantage and social exclusion have included studies of Greece (Tsakloglou and Panopoulou, 1998); the Netherlands (Muffels et al., 1992); Sweden (Hallerod, 1995); Ireland (Nolan and Whelan, 1996); and France (Paugam, 1995).

In general these are single country, rather than comparative, studies and there is a distinct lack of comparative work, and to a lesser degree national-level work, on multi-dimensional disadvantage. Part of the reason for this scarcity is the lack of genuinely comparable information on multi-dimensional disadvantage at a European level. To date much of the comparative work on poverty in Europe has focused on income. The introduction of the ECHP survey now makes such multi-dimensional comparisons possible.

THE EUROPEAN COMMUNITY HOUSEHOLD PANEL (ECHP) SURVEY

A Unique Cross-National Research Tool

The ECHP is a multi-dimensional and multi-purpose survey introduced in 1994 to yield information on the social dimension of the European Union. It was intended to contribute to the formulation and monitoring of policies across Europe in a variety of areas and to serve the needs of research, both inside and outside the European Commission.

The ECHP is a unique survey in many ways. Three of the most important characteristics of the survey are that: (1) it is comparable between participating countries of the European Union; (2) it is a panel survey and therefore allows longitudinal analysis to be performed; and (3) it is a multi-dimensional survey that covers a wide range of demographic, economic and social topics. These important characteristics are explained in more detail below.

Cross-National Comparability

The ECHP is the first survey to collect truly comparable dynamic information on a wide range of demographic, social and economic indicators across Europe. To allow accurate comparisons between countries, the survey is based on a harmonised questionnaire. This means that a core questionnaire is administered in each of the countries included in the survey. This questionnaire was designed centrally at Eurostat in close consultation with member states, particularly those who were already conducting their own panel surveys.

The use of a common instrument ensures not only common concepts and content for the surveys but also a common approach to their operationalisation and implementation. The development of a common questionnaire serves two main objectives in a multi-country survey like the ECHP. First, it defines the information to be provided by national surveys in precise terms, that is, it can be read as a list of variables to be produced. Secondly, the common information requirements elaborated in the form of an actual questionnaire help to standardise basic concepts, definitions and classifications to

Table 1.4   Countries included in the ECHP survey by year of inception

Year of inception	Country
Wave 1 (1994)	Belgium*
	Denmark
	France
	Germany
	Greece
	Ireland
	Italy
	Luxembourg
	Netherlands*
	Portugal
	Spain
	United Kingdom
Wave 2 (1995) additions	Austria

Note: *Have developed the ECHP as a continuation and adaptation of existing national panels.

be used, as well as the survey arrangements, methods of measurement and technical procedures such as editing and other data adjustments.

Nevertheless ECHP allows flexibility for adaptation to specific national circumstances which can vary considerably between the Member States. For example the questionnaire varies from the original quite considerably in Ireland, where there are extra questions to cover such topics as income from agriculture, and in France where the questionnaire has been modified to be more in line with other national surveys.

The first wave of the survey was conducted in 12 European countries and two extra countries joined the survey in the second wave a year later. The only EU country not to be included in the ECHP by the second wave of the survey was Sweden. Other European countries are not included in the survey because they are not members of the EU, such as Norway, Switzerland, Iceland, and eastern European countries. The countries included in the survey in the first two waves of the ECHP are shown in Table 1.4.

Panel Survey

The second quality of the ECHP is that it is a panel survey. This design allows the same individuals to be followed over time by re-interviewing original sample members (those in households selected for inclusion in

Table 1.5   Sample sizes: ECHP, wave 2, 1994

	Households	Individuals
Austria	3 382	7 441
Germany	4 134	7 958
Greece	5 220	12 271
Portugal	4 916	11 858
United Kingdom	4 548	8 391
Belgium	4 022	7 732
Denmark	3 224	5 504
France	6 722	13 306
Ireland	3 584	8 531
Italy	7 128	17 780
Luxembourg	962	1 968
Netherlands	5 110	9 151
Spain	6 522	16 276

the first wave of the survey) on a yearly basis. Original sample members who move, or form or join new households, are followed up at their new location. Children born to sample members and children who reach the age of 16 are automatically included as part of the survey population. In this manner the survey reflects demographic changes in the population and continues to remain representative of the population over time.[3]

Given that the ECHP is a panel survey, the importance of achieving good response rates cannot be overemphasised. This is particularly crucial for those who wish to perform longitudinal analysis, but is also important for cross-sectional analysis of any of the waves. Since a panel survey follows individual respondents over time, there is the danger that sample sizes will deplete as contact with respondents is lost or they choose to drop out. Attrition rates are particularly likely to be high during the first few years of a panel survey, with respondents tending to remain fairly faithful to the survey subsequently. Achieved sample sizes can also vary quite considerably among countries in the ECHP. The number of households and number of individuals (including children) for all countries in the second wave of the survey is presented in Table 1.5. The wave 2 samples fall short of the original panel samples collected a year earlier due to non-contact, non-response, failure to follow-up sample cases for other reasons and households ceasing to exist. These shortfalls are compensated for to some extent by the inclusion of new (split-off) households coming into the sample as a result of the movement of sample persons.

The cross-sectional household response rates[4] for wave 2 of the ECHP were relatively high, an average for all the countries of approximately 90 per cent (Verma, 1996). Just over half the non-response was because of refusals, with the remainder the result of non-contact and other reasons. Across countries, wave 2 cross-sectional response rates varied from 85 per cent in Belgium and the UK, to nearly 95 per cent in Denmark.

As with all surveys, non-response bias can occur when households and individuals who failed to respond to the survey are systematically different from those who do respond. This can result in biased estimates when the survey results are used to make generalisations regarding the whole population.

The normal method of compensating for survey non-response is to use weights that adjust the responding survey units for those which fail to respond. The ECHP applied this method in formulating non-response rates, which were combined with weights to account for design effects and to correct the distribution of households and individuals on variables such as age, sex, main activity status and other relevant characteristics. The design weights are introduced to compensate for differences in the probabilities of selection into the sample, the weights given to each household being inversely proportional to its probability of selection.

Multi-Dimensional Coverage

The third important characteristic of the ECHP survey is that it covers a wide range of demographic, economic and social topics (see Tables 1.6 and 1.7). The survey itself is administered in two stages. The first stage involves a household interview, covering topics related to the household as whole and answered by a reference person.[5] This is followed by a personal interview, which is administered to all individuals in the household 16 years of age and older.

Table 1.6   Socio-demographic information in the ECHP household and individual questionnaires

Household level	Individual level
Size of household	Sex
Composition of household	Age
	Marital status
	Number of children
	Education
	Citizenship

Table 1.7   Examples of domains and sub-domains of disadvantage in the ECHP household and individual questionnaires

Domain	Household level sub-domains	Individual level sub-domains
Financial	Total net annual income Sources of income Main source of income Ability to make ends meet Satisfaction with financial situation	Total net annual income Sources of income Main source of income
Basic needs and consumption	Access to basic household amenities Ability to afford basic needs Access to basic household durables	
Housing	Tenure Housing quality Perceived risk of crime or vandalism in the area	
Education		Highest level of completed education
Labour market		Main activity status Position in the labour market Unemployment
Health		Self-reported health status Limitations in daily activities due to health, illness or disability
Social relations		Frequency of contacts with family or friends Frequency of contacts with neighbours
Social participation		Membership of club or organisation

The household interview collects information on: household composition, including intra-household relationships; demographic information, including education, marital status and citizenship; housing, including costs, tenure and accommodation problems; income, including the household's major sources of income and various indicators of the household's financial situation (together with 'event-history' information on the household's receipt of social assistance in the previous 12 months); possession of non-monetary household items such as amenities, durables and necessities.

A wide range of topics are covered in the individual interview such as health, social relations, social responsibilities and the degree of satisfaction with various aspects of work and life. Two major areas are covered in considerable detail. These concern labour market activity and personal income of the individual. Information on labour market activity includes profiles of present and previous work or main activity (including event-history information on the person's main activity status in the previous 12 months), job-seeking for the unemployed and satisfaction with present job. Questions on personal income cover income from employment, self-employment, capital and savings interest, and benefits received in the past year.

The various indicators of disadvantage included in Table 1.7 cover many dimensions, although they by no means provide an exhaustive range of measures that can be combined to completely define multi-dimensional disadvantage, nor to indicate social exclusion. However these measures do provide indicators of important dimensions of social exclusion and of where social policies can be applied to encourage integration in society.

Data Reporting Conventions

Throughout the book, reporting of data follows Eurostat instructions that percentages based on unweighted numbers less than 20 cannot be reported (represented in tables by *); and percentages based on unweighted numbers between 20–49 should be highlighted (represented in tables by ( )).

SUMMARY

Initiatives taken by the European Community in the late 1980s and early 1990s have been instrumental in promoting the concept of social exclusion in social policy discourse and in making some progress in analysis (Berghman, 1995). However empirical investigations are few and far between, confirming the need, both from a research and policy perspective, for comparable information on social exclusion across different European countries.

The introduction of the ECHP survey has meant that information on the social, demographic and economic aspects of individuals in EU Member States is available in a truly comparable format for the first time. Such data allow the application of recent methodological advancements in poverty methodology, from the analysis of income distributions and poverty lines to correlations between various indicators of disadvantage, both monetary and non-monetary. The construction of such indicators of multidimensional disadvantage is crucial for the guiding and monitoring of policies designed to constrain and eradicate social exclusion in Europe.

In order to address the problem of social exclusion within the European Union, it is necessary to identify the groups of individuals most at risk. This book focuses on an understanding of multi-dimensional disadvantage for four such potentially 'high' risk groups of individuals – young adults, lone parents, sick or disabled people and retired people. A chapter of the book is dedicated to each risk group, describing the demographic and policy context of each country in relation to findings on multi-dimensional disadvantage both within and between countries.

NOTES

1. The project was funded under the Framework Four programme for research and technological development. This Programme included all European Commission research and development work, covering areas such as information technology, environment, life sciences, energy and transport and the area of 'targeted socio-economic research', which is where this project was placed.
2. Given the demand for ECHP data and statistics from both inside and outside the European Commission, Eurostat constructed a users database in 1997. This database was designed as a user-friendly longitudinal database, with a set of rules allowing access to the data without jeopardising the necessary conditions of data confidentiality – the so-called EU 'statistical law'. Access is restricted by means of contracts stipulating the conditions of use, a general procedure adopted with most other survey databases. An ECHP user database containing waves 1–4 longitudinal files should be ready by December 2000. For information on the ECHP visit the Eurostat web site at http://europa.eu.int/eurostat.html.
3. The dynamic aspect of the ECHP must not be understated, particularly considering the role time plays in the conceptual definition of social exclusion. Building on the operationalisation of static indicators of social exclusion detailed in this book, our project also looks at the relationship between different measures of social exclusion in a dynamic context. This analysis includes the correlation between changes in different dimensions of disadvantage, an examination of the relevance of alternative measures of household resources to understanding the nature of social exclusion, and an investigation into the factors that can increase the likelihood of individuals and households moving towards or away from social exclusion.
4. Wave 2 cross-sectional household response rates are calculated as the ratio of the number of interviews completed to the number 'eligible' in the wave. For wave 2 eligible means the number of households forwarded from wave 1, less those which were no longer eligible or existing by the time of wave 2, plus split-off households newly coming into the sample.
5. The reference person must be normally resident at the household and is defined as the head of household if s/he is economically active (working or looking for work) or if there is no economically active person in the household. Otherwise the reference person is the spouse/partner of the head (if s/he is economically active) or, if none of these conditions are satisfied, the oldest economically active person in the household.

2. Poverty, material deprivation and multi-dimensional disadvantage during four life stages: evidence from the ECHP

Panos Tsakloglou and Fotis Papadopoulos

INTRODUCTION

The aim of this chapter is to examine the living standards of the four population groups ('risk groups', in the terminology used in this chapter's tables and graphs) that are the focus of this book, in comparison with the living standards of the entire population. These groups are: retired persons (Retired), sick or disabled persons (Sick), young adults (Young adults) and lone parents (Lone parents) as defined in Chapter 1. For this purpose, detailed analysis was undertaken of their average incomes, levels of poverty, housing amenities, ability to afford particular durable goods and necessities of life, as well as the impact of public transfers. The analysis of the living standards of specific sub-groups within these groups is presented in subsequent chapters.

Unlike the interpretations of the term 'social exclusion' provided by various social scientists, as outlined in Chapter 1, in the jargon of most policy makers in the EU social exclusion is used interchangeably in order to denote 'acute poverty and multiple deprivation' or 'exclusion from the labour market'. The analysis described here aims to identify aspects of the risk of social exclusion that are closer to the first of these interpretations. The data used for the analysis come from the second wave of the European Community Household Panel (ECHP) that was described in Chapter 1. It can be argued that although the ECHP is much better suited for the analysis of the phenomenon of social exclusion than most other existing data sources in EU member states, it still leaves a lot to be desired. A number of aspects of social exclusion cannot be analysed at all or can be analysed only to a limited extent using the ECHP (for example, neighbourhood effects, relational aspects, issues related to race or ethnicity, and so on). Further, the fact that the ECHP is still a 'young' panel, restricts our ability to examine in depth dynamic aspects of multiple deprivation and social exclusion.

The remainder of this chapter is organised as follows. The next section is devoted to a comparison of the levels of monetary poverty of the four groups with those of the rest of the population and also deals with a number of methodological issues. The third section covers issues of non-monetary deprivation and multi-dimensional disadvantage, while the fourth examines the extent to which social transfers prevent the members of the risk groups from falling below the poverty line. Finally, some tentative conclusions are provided regarding the overall living standards of the four risk groups in comparison with the rest of the population.

POVERTY

In the first attempt to compare the risk of material deprivation of the four groups with that of the rest of the population, their relative poverty risks are examined. For the purposes of this comparison distributions of equivalent income per capita are used. The concept of income chosen is 'net monetary household income'. This is made up of all wages and salaries, incomes from self-employment (including farming), capital income (that is, income from investment, savings, insurance or property), private transfers, pensions and other social transfers net of income taxes and social insurance contributions received from all household members.

Distributions of net monetary income are frequently used in cross-country comparative inequality and poverty studies.[1] However, for a number of reasons, they may be far from ideal for such purposes. The main reason for an interest in the measurement of poverty may be to be able to evaluate the welfare position of the least well off members of a society. However, 'welfare' is not directly observable and therefore, for the purposes of empirical analysis, a reasonably close approximation to it has to be used instead. Several economists and other social scientists argue that, ceteris paribus, an individual's welfare level is determined by his/her levels of consumption and leisure. Since there are enormous difficulties in evaluating leisure in monetary terms, most empirical poverty studies use disposable income or, to a lesser extent, consumption expenditure as indicators of welfare. Each variable has its merits from a theoretical point of view (Haveman, 1990; Atkinson, 1991; Sen, 1992; Chaudhuri and Ravallion, 1994). Nevertheless, irrespective of whether disposable income or consumption expenditure is used as a welfare indicator, it would be desirable to utilise concepts of resources that are as close as possible to the notion of

'command over resources' and, hence, which include income in kind from
private sources evaluated at market prices, as well as the value of goods
and services provided free of charge by the State. Otherwise, comparisons
between countries with different degrees of monetisation of their economies, institutional frameworks or types of welfare state may be problematic. Furthermore, comparisons within countries may also be problematic
if particular population groups rely more heavily than others on incomes
in kind and/or are heavier users of goods and services provided by the State.
The evidence of Smeeding et al. (1993) suggests that the inclusion of non-
cash public transfers in the fields of health, education and housing in the
concept of resources in seven countries – four of them EU member states
– results in a decline in measured inequality and poverty (in comparison
with the estimates of inequality and poverty indices derived from the distribution of monetary income). Likewise, the inclusion of private incomes
in kind in the concept of resources results in a substantial decline in measured inequality and poverty in Greece.[2] Since the concept of resources that
is available in the ECHP and used in this book is 'net monetary household
income', the above limitations should be kept in mind when interpreting the
results reported below.

The distributions used in this section are distributions of equivalent
income per capita.[3] They are derived by dividing the sum of the incomes of
all household members by the number of equivalent adults in the household and then assigning the resulting figure to each household member.
Equivalence scales are used in distributional studies in order to take into
account two factors: household economies of scale in consumption and,
sometimes, differences in needs between adults and children. The scales
used in the main part of the analysis are the so-called 'modified OECD
scales' (Hagenaars et al., 1994) which assign a weight of one to the first
adult in the household, a weight of 0.5 to all other household members
aged 14 or more and a weight of 0.3 to each child (person aged below 14).
In comparison with other sets of equivalence scales frequently used in distributional studies, these scales imply moderate household economies of
scale (Buhmann et al., 1988). It should be noted that the selection of a particular set of equivalence scales may not be 'innocuous' with respect to
welfare comparisons across different population groups. This can be illustrated with examples related to two of the groups used in our analysis.
'Retired' and 'Lone parents' are disproportionately found in households
whose size is smaller than average. Therefore, if the equivalence scales used
in the analysis imply low (high) household economies of scale,[4] then, ceteris
paribus, the mean equivalent income per capita of these groups will
increase (decrease) and their poverty rate decline (rise) relative to the
national mean. On the other hand, lone parent households are likely to

contain more children than the average household. Hence, if the equivalence scales used in the analysis imply low costs of children relative to adults, the mean equivalent income per capita of the group will rise and the poverty rate decline relative to the national average. For this reason, in this chapter a sensitivity analysis is performed in order to test the robustness of findings with respect to the use of alternative sets of equivalence scales. For the purposes of this sensitivity analysis a family of two-parameter equivalence scales is used, which parameterises simultaneously both the household economies of scale and the costs of children relative to the costs of adults (Johnson and Garner (1995).[5]

The poverty line used in the main part of the analysis is that used by Eurostat, which adopts a relativistic approach to the measurement of poverty and fixes the poverty line at a level equal to 60 per cent of the median equivalent income of the population. Since most income distributions are approximately lognormal (that is, skewed to the right), the proportion of the population falling below the poverty line is likely to be very sensitive to the selection of a particular poverty line. This may not have particular implications for the analysis *per se*, unless certain population groups are likely to be disproportionately concentrated in particular sections of the income distribution. Indeed, this may be the case with some of the groups of interest in this analysis (for example, 'Retired' relying on minimum pensions, or 'Lone parents' or 'Sick' relying on particular social transfers). For this reason, a sensitivity analysis is performed, by setting the poverty line successively at the 50 per cent, 60 per cent and 70 per cent of the median equivalent income and examining the relative position of the four risk groups.

The main poverty index used in our analysis is the poverty rate (proportion of the population falling below the poverty line). However informative and easy to understand the poverty rate may be, it has a number of well-known disadvantages. It does not show how poor the poor are (their average distance from the poverty line) and, further, it does not provide any information about income distribution among the poor. For this reason, a number of poverty indices have been developed since the seminal article of Sen (1976) which do not suffer from these disadvantages. One such index is that developed by Foster et al. (1984), which is also 'additively decomposable'; that is, it allows the quantification of each group's contribution to aggregate poverty. Estimates of this index are also included in some of the tables in this chapter.[6]

Before proceeding to a detailed examination of the poverty situation of the four risk groups, it is important to examine their position in the entire income distribution of the five countries covered by our analysis. This is done in the graphs of Figure 2.1. For the purposes of the graphs of the two

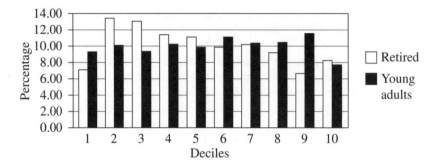

Figure 2.1a   Austria – Risk groups per decile

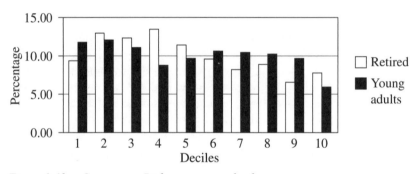

Figure 2.1b   Germany – Risk groups per decile

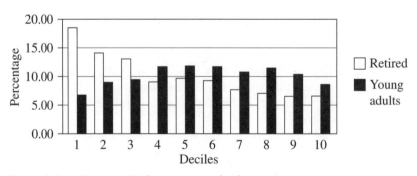

Figure 2.1c   Greece – Risk groups per decile

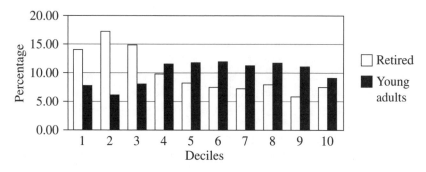

Figure 2.1d   Portugal – Risk groups per decile

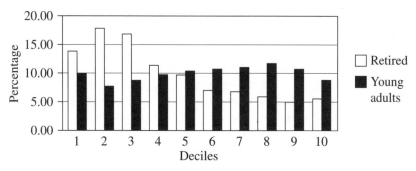

Figure 2.1e   UK – Risk groups per decile

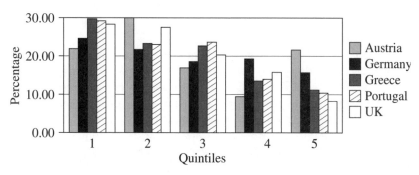

Figure 2.1f   Sick/disabled per quintile

largest risk groups – 'Young adults' and 'Retired' – the total population of each country is ordered according to their equivalent income from the poorest to the richest and then grouped into ten groups of equal size (deciles). Due to small cell sizes the group of 'Sick/disabled' is grouped in quintiles. Finally, in the case of 'Lone parents' because of extremely small cell sizes (less than 20 cases) in the highest income deciles (quintiles) no graph is presented; only a description of their income distribution. The graphs report the distribution of the four risk groups per decile for each country. If the income distribution of a particular group is exactly the same as that of the entire population, then 10 per cent of its members should belong to each decile (20 per cent in the case of quintiles). The more the members of a particular group are concentrated close to the bottom of the distribution, the lower the group's average welfare and the higher its poverty risk.[7]

In Austria the 'Retired' appear to be over-represented in the bottom half of the distribution, but not at the lowest decile. In contrast, 'Young adults' are slightly over-represented in the top half of the distribution, though not at the top decile. The two risk groups that are clearly disproportionately concentrated close to the bottom of the distribution are the 'Sick' and, particularly, the 'Lone parents'.

The situation of the 'Retired' in Germany appears to be similar to that in Austria. 'Young adults' and 'Sick/disabled' are over-represented in the three poorest deciles (in the bottom two quintiles). The risk group that is most concentrated in the bottom half of the distribution and, especially, the two lowest deciles is the 'Lone parents'.

The overall picture of the risk groups in Greece is rather different from those of Austria and Germany. The risk group that appears to be most clearly over-represented in the bottom half of the distribution is the 'Retired', followed by the 'Sick'. Perhaps due to small numbers, the distribution of 'Lone parents' appears to be rather erratic, although they also seem to be more concentrated close to the bottom of the distribution. Unlike the other groups, 'Young adults' are over-represented in the upper–middle part of the distribution.

'Retired', 'Sick' and 'Lone parents' are over-represented in the three poorest deciles (bottom two quintiles) of the Portuguese income distribution. Nevertheless, the distribution of 'Lone parents' has some elements of bimodality and the members of this group are also over-represented at the top end of the distribution (particularly in the richest decile). Like Greece, 'Young adults' in Portugal are concentrated in the upper–middle part of the income distribution (though not the top decile) and they are under-represented in the three poorest deciles.

The risk group that is overwhelmingly concentrated in the three lowest deciles of the United Kingdom's income distribution is 'Lone parents'. 'Retired' and 'Sick' are also disproportionately concentrated in the bottom half of the income distribution while, as in the other countries, 'Young adults' seem to be slightly over-represented in the upper–middle part of the distribution.

Next the first two lines of Table 2.1. give an overview of the overall poverty picture in the five countries under consideration. Using the 'modified OECD equivalence scales' and a poverty line equal to 60 per cent of the median equivalent income, the five countries can be grouped into two groups according to their poverty rates. The poverty rates of Austria (AT), Germany (D) and the United Kingdom (UK) cluster around 16.0 per cent to 17.5 per cent, whereas the corresponding rates of Greece (GR) and Portugal (PT) are substantially higher – 21.7 per cent and 23.4 per cent, respectively. Cross-country differences appear to be even higher when the Foster et al. index is used so that the depth and the intensity of poverty are taken into account, along with its prevalence. In this case, aggregate poverty in the United Kingdom appears to be substantially lower than in Austria and Germany which, in turn, have considerably lower poverty levels than Greece and Portugal.

Table 2.1   Aggregate poverty and populations' shares of four risk groups in five EU member states

	AT	D	GR	PT	UK
Poverty rate	15.9	16.2	21.7	23.4	17.4
Foster et al. index ($\times 1000$)	23.6	25.5	37.1	38.8	17.5
Population share 'Retired'	26.5	29.0	30.4	22.8	25.6
Population share 'Sick'	2.9	3.6	2.5	5.4	3.6
Population share 'Young adults'	25.8	18.2	21.7	24.1	21.0
Population share 'Lone parents'	1.5	1.6	0.8	1.4	3.3

The last four lines of Table 2.1 report the population shares of the four risk groups in each of the five countries. Other things being equal, these shares can give a rough idea of the potential importance of these groups in each country's public policy discourse. The 'Retired', whose definition combines both occupational and demographic elements, are the largest of the four risk groups in all countries, apart from Portugal. Cross-country differences with respect to this group's population share appear to be large in absolute but not in relative terms. Their population share varies between 22.8 per cent in Portugal and 30.4 per cent in Greece. The population share of the 'Sick', whose definition is the only one that relies solely on self-reported information, varies considerably across countries – from 2.5 per cent in Greece to 5.4 per cent in Portugal. The 'Young adults' are the second largest risk group in all countries apart from Portugal (where they are the largest group). As in the case of the 'Retired', cross-country differences in the population shares of the 'Young adults' appear to be quite large in absolute terms but less so in relative terms. In Austria their population share is the highest, 25.8 per cent, whereas in Germany it is the lowest, 18.2 per cent. The most important cross-country differences in population shares are recorded in the case of 'Lone parents'. Their population share in the United Kingdom is as high as 3.3 per cent, whereas in Greece it is less than 1 per cent (0.8 per cent).[8] In the three other countries it is around 1.5 per cent.

Table 2.2[9] provides a group-by-group detailed analysis of the poverty situation of the four risk groups. The first column reports the mean equivalent income of each group in each country as a proportion of the national mean (national mean: 100). Likewise, the second and the third columns of the table report estimates of the poverty rate and the Foster et al. index in comparison with the corresponding national means.[10] Values higher (lower) than 1.00 denote a higher (lower) poverty risk for the members of the risk groups than those faced by the average population member. The last two columns of the table examine the robustness of the findings to alternative specifications of the poverty line and the equivalence scale. More specifically, in the case of poverty lines, the estimates of the poverty rate and the Foster et al. index of each group are compared with the corresponding estimates for the entire population of the country under consideration, when the poverty line is successively set at 50 per cent, 60 per cent and 70 per cent of the median equivalent income (six comparisons per group). A 'Yes' ('No') in the column 'Poverty line sensitivity' implies that the results reported in the second and third column of the table are sensitive (robust) with respect to the selection of any of these poverty lines. In other words, the relative position of the risk group changes (does not change) *vis-à-vis* the entire population, when the poverty line is set at a different level. Similarly, the last column of the table examines the sensitivity of the estimates reported in the second and the third column, when alternative parameters regarding household economies of scale and relative costs of adults and children are utilised (twelve comparisons per group). A 'Yes' ('No') in the column 'Equivalence scale sensitivity' means that the results reported in the second and third column of the table are sensitive (robust) with respect to the choice of any of these equivalence scales. In other words, the relative position of the risk group changes (does not change) in comparison with the entire population, when another equivalence scale is selected.

Table 2.2   Poverty comparisons of risk groups

Country per cent risk group	Mean equivalent income (all: 100.0)	Poverty rate (relative) (all: 1.00)	Foster et al. (relative) (all: 1.00)	Poverty line sensitivity	Equivalence scale sensitivity
Retired					
AT	95.1	0.96	0.77	YES[1]	YES
D	93.0	1.05	0.88	YES[2]	YES
GR	81.9	1.60	1.76	NO	NO
PT	84.1	1.59	1.16	YES[3]	NO
UK	79.7	1.55	1.37	NO	NO
Sick					
AT	94.8	[1.15]	[1.08]	NO	NO
D	92.6	[1.22]	[1.51]	NO	NO
GR	81.8	1.47	1.31	NO	NO
PT	77.9	1.36	1.47	NO	NO
UK	76.8	1.26	1.60	NO	NO
Young adults					
AT	97.9	0.96	0.77	NO	YES[5]
D	91.5	1.19	1.08	NO	YES
GR	99.6	0.78	0.70	NO	NO
PT	101.3	0.73	0.82	NO	NO
UK	99.9	0.87	0.95	NO	NO
Lone parents					
AT	76.2	[1.88]	[1.36]	NO	NO
D	73.8	2.46	1.81	NO	NO
GR	94.1	[1.65]	[1.10]	YES[4]	NO
PT	92.3	1.46	1.51	NO	NO
UK	59.9	2.82	2.47	NO	NO

Notes:
1. Re-ranking by Head count ratio at the 70 per cent poverty line only.
2. Re-ranking by Head count ratio at the 50 per cent poverty line only.
3. Re-ranking by the FGT index at the 50 per cent poverty line only.
4. Re-ranking by the FGT index at the 50 per cent poverty line only.
5. Marginal difference.

The mean equivalent income of the 'Retired' is lower than the national average in all countries under examination. However, cross-country differences are considerable. In the United Kingdom the mean income of the 'Retired' is less than 80 per cent of the national mean, in Austria it is over 95 per cent. Low mean incomes for the 'Retired' in comparison with the national average are also observed in Portugal and Greece, whereas their situation appears to be considerably better in Germany. The proportion of the 'Retired' who fall below the poverty line is higher than the national average in all countries but Austria. However, when the depth and intensity of poverty are also taken into account using the Foster et al. index, poverty among the 'Retired' in Germany as well as in Austria appears to be less acute than in the entire population.[11] These results are strengthened further by the results reported in the last two columns of the table. The result that poverty is more acute among the 'Retired' than among the rest of the population is robust to alternative specifications of the poverty line and the equivalence scale in the United Kingdom, Greece and (almost) Portugal. On the contrary, in Austria and Germany the relative poverty situation of the 'Retired' depends on the particular poverty line and equivalence scale used.

Unlike the 'Retired', the group of 'Sick' appears by all monetary indicators to be worse off than the rest of the population. In all countries the mean equivalent income of the group is lower and the risk of poverty higher than that for the rest of the population. The latter is robust to alternative specifications of the poverty line and the equivalence scale. However, in absolute terms cross-country differences appear to be substantial. For example, the group's mean income in Austria is 94.8 per cent of the national mean, whereas in the United Kingdom it is only 76.8 per cent.

With the possible exception of Germany, in the countries under examination the mean equivalent income of the 'Young adults' is very close to the national average. According to the poverty estimates reported in the second and the third column of the table, it appears that in all countries apart from Germany the poverty risk of this group is lower than the national average – sometimes substantially so. Furthermore, this result appears to be robust to alternative specifications of the poverty line and the equivalence scale in Greece, Portugal, the United Kingdom and (almost) Austria. On the contrary, the relative poverty status of the German 'Young adults' in comparison with the rest of the population varies, depending on the equivalence scale used.

The last panel of Table 2.2 demonstrates that of the four risk groups, in most cases, it is the group of 'Lone parents' that runs the highest risk of poverty. In all countries the mean income of this group is lower than the national average, but the cross-country differences are very significant. The corresponding figures are between 90–95 per cent of the national mean in Greece and Portugal, around 75 per cent in Austria and Germany and lower than 60 per cent in the United Kingdom. Moreover, estimates of the poverty indices for the group are considerably higher than the national average, especially in the case of the United Kingdom and, to a lesser extent, Germany. In particular in the United Kingdom these estimates are between two and three times the national average. With a marginal exception in the case of Greece, in all countries these results are not sensitive with respect to the choice of poverty lines or equivalence scales.

Naturally, one may question whether the real poverty-inducing factor is the participation in one of the risk groups rather than other factors associated with these groups that have not been taken into account in the above analysis. For this reason, a multivariate analysis was carried out. More specifically, for each country a logit model was estimated of the probability of falling below the poverty line, for the group of persons aged 16 or more. The explanatory variables used were dummy variables denoting participation in one of the four risk groups as well as employment status, household type and educational status of the individual, and employment status and educational level of the reference person of the individual's household.[12] The resulting marginal effects from the participation in one of the risk groups in comparison with the reference group (impact effects), along with the statistical significance of the corresponding coefficients are reported in Table 2.3. Some of the results, especially those related to the group of 'Retired' should be interpreted with caution, since this variable is relatively highly correlated with a number of other variables included in the regression equation.

A number of the results reported in Table 2.3 are very interesting. Other things being equal, in all countries under consideration being a member of a lone-parent household increases dramatically the probability of falling

Table 2.3   Marginal effects and statistical significance of risk variables in multinomial logit analysis[1]

	AT	D	GR	PT	UK
Retired	8.9**	0.7	8.4**	9.0**	3.2*
Sick	1.9	3.5	6.0**	2.1*	−1.6
Young adults	−1.0	1.0	4.2**	0.9	0.5
Lone parents	22.3**	17.3**	27.1**	19.6**	18.3**

Notes:
1. Change in percentage points of the risk of falling below the poverty line in comparison with the reference group
Reference group: Employees, with less than upper secondary education completed, living in households consisting of couples with one or more children (at least one >16), headed by employees with less than upper secondary education completed. (Regional effects controlled in all countries except Germany.)
** Derived from a coefficient statistically significant at the 1 per cent level.
 * Derived from a coefficient statistically significant at the 5 per cent level.

below the poverty line. The corresponding impact effects are highly significant and vary between 17.3 per cent in Germany and 27.1 per cent in Greece.[13] Further, being a member of the 'Retired' group increases significantly the risk of poverty in all countries apart from Germany. In three countries (Austria, Greece and Portugal) the corresponding impact effects are 8–9 per cent, while the relevant effect for the United Kingdom is significant at conventional levels of statistical significance, but substantially smaller (3.2 per cent). Participation in one of the remaining 'risk groups' increases significantly the probability of falling below the poverty line only in Greece ('Sick' by 6.0 per cent and, surprisingly, 'Young adults' by 4.2 per cent) and Portugal ('Sick' by 2.1 per cent).[14]

NON-MONETARY MATERIAL DEPRIVATION AND MULTI-DIMENSIONAL DISADVANTAGE

One of the main advantages of using the ECHP for the purposes of the present analysis is that it provides the opportunity to examine simultaneously monetary and non-monetary aspects of deprivation. This section is devoted to the examination of non-monetary aspects of material deprivation of the four risk groups in comparison with the rest of the population. Three aspects of relative deprivation are explored: deprivation in terms of housing conditions, durable goods and household necessities.

With respect to housing conditions, the ECHP contains the following information. First, whether the dwelling of the individual's household has the following amenities:

1. a separate kitchen;
2. a bath or shower;
3. an indoor flushing toilet;
4. hot running water;
5. central heating or electric storage heaters; and
6. a place to sit outside (for example terrace or garden).

Secondly, whether the household has any of the following problems with its accommodation (self-reported information):

1. shortage of space;
2. noise from neighbours or outside;
3. being too dark or not having enough light;
4. lack of adequate heating facilities;
5. leaky roof;

6. damp walls, floors, foundation, etc;
7. rot in window frames or floors;
8. pollution, grime or other environmental problems caused by traffic or industry; and
9. vandalism or crime in the area.

In order to aggregate the above information in a single indicator of deprivation in the field of housing conditions, it was decided to adopt a different approach to that adopted by a number of researchers using the ECHP or similar data sets who, effectively, assign the same weight to the lack of every item.[15] More specifically, our 'housing conditions deprivation indicator' assigns to each population member whose household is lacking one of the above housing amenities or facing one of the above problems a weight equal to the proportion of the population living in dwellings not lacking the corresponding amenity or not reporting the relevant problem. As a result, if a particular problem is very rare (common) in one country, an individual whose household is facing this problem is given a high (low) weight. Then, the weights of each population member are added and divided by the sum of the average 'satisfaction' score in the entire population (that is, the sum of the proportions of the population not lacking particular housing amenities or not reporting particular housing problems).[16]

Regarding durable goods, the ECHP contains information on enforced lack[17] of the following goods:

1. a car or van (available for private use);
2. a colour TV;
3. a video recorder;
4. a microwave oven;
5. a dishwasher;
6. a telephone; and
7. a second home.

An indicator of deprivation (enforced lack) in the field of durable goods was constructed using a methodology identical to the one outlined above for the construction of the 'housing conditions deprivation indicator'.[18]

Finally, with respect to household necessities ('necessities of life'), the reference person of each household in the sample of the ECHP was asked to report whether the household could afford (if they wished to):

1. to keep the home adequately warm;
2. to pay for a week's annual holiday away from home;
3. to replace worn-out furniture;

4. to buy new, rather than second-hand, clothes;
5. to eat meat, chicken or fish every second day; and
6. to have friends or family for a drink or meal at least once a month.

This information was also aggregated into a single 'household necessities deprivation indicator' using the methodology outlined above.

The first three lines of Table 2.4 provide the aggregate picture for the five countries, reporting the average deprivation score in each area (housing conditions, consumer durables and household necessities). A clear picture of two distinct groups of countries emerges from these figures. On the one side are the poorer countries, Portugal and Greece, with relatively high deprivation scores and on the other side the richer ones, Austria, Germany and the United Kingdom, with substantially lower deprivation scores in all three areas.

Furthermore, the ECHP contains information on subjective evaluation of well-being. The reference person of each household was asked to report whether the household's total income was sufficient to make ends meet. The replies were given in a six point scale ('with great difficulty' (6), 'with difficulty' (5), 'with some difficulty' (4), 'fairly easily' (3), 'easily' (2), and 'very easily' (1)). This information is analysed in the last two lines of Table 2.4. These lines show, first, the proportion of the population in each country living in households reporting that they make ends meet 'with great difficulty' and, secondly, the average subjective evaluation of well-being score, according to the above scale – admittedly a very crude but, nonetheless, informative indicator. The estimates reported in the lower panel of Table 2.4 seem to be broadly in line with the previous findings of this chapter. More specifically, two groups of countries can be distinguished. The first group consists of Greece and Portugal where considerable proportions of the population live in households reporting that they have great

Table 2.4   Aggregate non-monetary deprivation indicators in five EU member states

	AT	D	GR	PT	UK
Housing conditions	8.7	5.0	10.4	15.1	2.4
Consumer durables	5.0	4.6	15.5	23.4	4.7
Household necessities	14.4	10.2	43.4	34.1	15.3
Subjective evaluation of well-being ('great difficulty' %)	6.1	2.2	20.4	15.4	5.2
Subjective evaluation of well-being ('average score')	3.5	2.8	4.5	4.3	3.4

difficulties in making ends meet. In contrast, in the countries of the second group relatively low proportions of the population live in households reporting such acute difficulties (Austria, the United Kingdom and, particularly, Germany).[19]

Like Table 2.2 in the case of monetary deprivation (poverty), Table 2.5 provides a group-by-group detailed analysis of the relative situation of the four risk groups with respect to their average non-monetary material deprivation. This time, however, the notation is slightly different, for expositional reasons. Instead of presenting estimates as ratios of the national means (100), we report relative deprivation risks, μ, as 'close to the national average', $95 < \mu < 105$ (=), 'moderately high' $105 < \mu < 125$ (+), 'moderately low' $75 < \mu < 95$ (−), 'high' $125 < \mu < 150$ (++), 'low' $50 < \mu < 75$ (−−), 'very high' $150 < (+++)$ and 'very low' $\mu < 50$ (−−−). The first three columns report relative deprivation risks for housing conditions, consumer durables and household necessities ('necessities of life'), respectively. The last two columns report the proportion of the risk group reporting 'great difficulties in making ends meet' and the group's average 'well-being score' in comparison with the corresponding national means.

The first panel of Table 2.5 suggests that in all countries the dwellings of the 'Retired' are not as well equipped in terms of housing amenities as those of the rest of the population – less so in Austria and Germany. The picture is mixed with respect to their ability to afford durable goods. In two countries – Germany and, especially, Austria – the corresponding average deprivation scores are lower than the national mean, in Greece and the United Kingdom they are close to the national average and only in Portugal the corresponding relative risk appears to be moderately high. In terms of relative deprivation in the field of household necessities, the 'Retired' appear to run a moderately high risk of relative deprivation in three countries (Austria, Portugal and the United Kingdom), whereas in Germany their index is close to the national average and in Greece they appear to face a high risk of relative deprivation. Some very interesting results are reported in the last two columns of this panel. In spite of the fact that in at least three countries (Greece, Portugal and the United Kingdom) the 'Retired' appear to be worse off in comparison with the rest of the population in both monetary and non-monetary terms, their average score in the subjective evaluation of well-being question is very close to the national mean. Moreover, in the United Kingdom the proportion of the 'Retired' who live in households reporting 'great difficulties in making ends meet' is substantially lower than the national average. Similar results are also reported in Austria and Germany. Therefore, at least some of the results of the last two columns of the first panel of Table 2.5 may seem surprising and, perhaps, counterintuitive. The explanation may lie in the life aspirations of the various population groups. The 'Retired' are substantially older than the average population member and belong to a generation that, on average, enjoyed substantially lower living standards than the younger generations. Hence they may not feel deprived, even in cases where their living standards lag seriously behind those of the rest of the population.

The information reported in the second panel of Table 2.5 suggests that, unlike the 'Retired', the position of the 'Sick' is substantially worse than that of the rest of the population in both 'objective' and 'subjective' terms. In all countries their risk of relative deprivation in terms of housing amenities is either moderately high or high whereas, with very few exceptions, their relative deprivation scores in terms of consumer durables and household necessities are high or very high. Likewise, in all countries the proportion of the 'Sick' living in households reporting 'great difficulties in making ends meet' is substantially higher than the national average and their average score on the subjective evaluation of well-being question is lower than the national mean.

A mixed picture emerges from Table 2.5 regarding the relative position of the group of 'Young adults'. With respect to housing amenities their relative deprivation scores in three countries (Austria, Greece and Portugal) are slightly lower than the national average and in two (Germany and the United Kingdom) slightly higher. However, with the exceptions of Portugal and, partly, Greece, the 'Young adults' live in households reporting high relative deprivation scores regarding their ability to afford durable goods whereas their differences from the national means are not very high with respect to deprivation in terms of household necessities. Nevertheless, the proportion of 'Young adults' living in households reporting great difficulties in making ends meet, are (moderately) higher than the national average, with the exception of Portugal (close to the national average) and the United Kingdom (higher than the national average). Further, in Austria and the United Kingdom their average score on the subjective evaluation of well-being question is moderately lower than the national average.

In terms of housing amenities deprivation, the situation of the 'Lone parents' varies substantially across countries. In Germany, their relative deprivation score is very high, whereas in Greece it appears to be low. In the remaining countries, it does not differ considerably from the national average. However, the picture changes dramatically for the relative deprivation risks of this group in terms of consumer durable goods and household necessities. The corresponding relative deprivation scores are very high in Austria, Germany and, especially, the United Kingdom, high in Greece and moderately high in Portugal. Furthermore, in all countries the proportion of 'Lone parents' living in households reporting great difficulties in making ends meet is dramatically higher and their average scores on the subjective

Table 2.5 Comparisons of 'risk groups' in terms of material non-monetary deprivation indicators (national average: 100)

Country per cent risk group	Housing conditions	Consumer durables	Household necessities	Subjective evaluation of well-being ('great difficulty' %)	Subjective evaluation of well-being ('average score')
Retired					
AT	+	− −	+	−	=
D	+	−	=	− −	=
GR	+ +	=	+ +	+	=
PT	+ +	+	+	+	=
UK	+ +	=	+	− −	=
Sick					
AT	+	+ +	+ + +	+ + +	+
D	+ +	+ +	+ + +	+ + +	+
GR	+ +	+	+ +	+ + +	+
PT	+	+ +	+ +	+ + +	+
UK	+ +	+ + +	+ + +	+ + +	+
Young Adults					
AT	−	+ +	=	+	+
D	+	+ +	+	+	=
GR	−	+	−	=	=
PT	−	=	=	+	=
UK	+	+ +	+	+ +	+
Lone parents					
AT	=	+ + +	+ + +	+ + +	+ +
D	+ + +	+ + +	+ + +	+ + +	+ +
GR	− −	+ +	+ +	+ + +	+
PT	+	+	+	+ + +	+
UK	=	+ + +	+ + +	+ + +	+ +

Notes:
  −: 75 < μ < 95
  =: 95 < μ < 105
  +: 105 < μ < 125
 − −: 50 < μ < 75
 + +: 125 < μ < 150
− − −:   μ < 50
+ + +: 150 < μ

evaluation of well-being question lower than the corresponding national averages.

The next issue to be investigated is the extent to which the various types of deprivation analysed above are correlated; in other words, the extent of multidimensional disadvantage is examined in the risk groups, as well as in the entire population. This is done in Tables 2.6 and 2.7. In Table 2.6 a thoroughgoing relativistic approach is adopted. Population members are identified as 'deprived' if they are in the bottom quintile of the distribution of the relevant deprivation indices (housing conditions, consumer durables and household necessities). Then, a count is made of the number of criteria on which each population member is classified as deprived. Finally, the proportions of the four risk groups, as well as the corresponding proportions in the entire population of each country, who are classified as deprived according to none, at least one, at least two and all three criteria in each country are reported in the panels of the table. Comparison of the estimates for the entire population with the estimates for the risk groups provides a rough idea of the relative risk of multidimensional disadvantage for the members of these groups.

The evidence in Table 2.6 shows that in Austria and Germany, the risk groups that face a high risk of multi-dimensional disadvantage in comparison with the rest of the population are the 'Sick' and the 'Lone parents'. Especially in Germany and the UK, 'Lone parents' are over three times more likely than the average population member to be deprived in at least two categories of relative deprivation examined here. In both countries, the relative position of the 'Retired' and the 'Young adults' is not substantially different from that of the rest of the population. In Greece, in addition to the 'Sick' and 'Lone parents', the 'Retired' also face a high risk of multi-dimensional disadvantage. In contrast, this risk is lower than the national average for the group of 'Young adults'. The Portuguese situation is very similar to that in Greece; 'Sick' 'Lone parents' and 'Retired' face a higher risk of multi-dimensional disadvantage than the average population member, while 'Young adults' do not. The only country in which all the risk groups seem to face a higher risk of multi-dimensional disadvantage than the rest of the population is the United Kingdom. Among the risk groups, the ones that seem to face an extremely high risk are the 'Sick' and, particularly, the 'Lone parents'. It is worth noting that, even though over two-thirds of the British population are not classified as deprived according to any of the criteria used for the purposes of Table 2.6, the corresponding proportion is only one quarter in the case of 'Lone parents'.

Another interesting issue that is investigated in Table 2.6 is the extent to which monetary and non-monetary aspects of deprivation are correlated. The last line of each panel reports the proportion of the persons who are

Table 2.6 *Comparisons of 'risk groups' in terms of aggregate material non-monetary deprivation indicators (bottom 20 per cent of the distribution)*

Country per cent risk group	Deprived according to:*			
	No criterion	At least one criterion	At least two criteria	All three criteria
AT				
Retired	49.3	50.7	17.0	3.8
Sick	46.4	53.6	24.8	*
Adults	52.1	47.9	17.9	3.0
Lone parents	[40.8]	59.2	[25.2]	*
TOTAL POPULATION	55.1	44.9	15.7	3.5
% in bottom quintile**	13.3	24.6	32.6	33.6
D				
Retired	59.6	40.4	10.3	[1.1]
Sick	46.8	53.2	20.0	*
Adults	55.2	44.8	15.2	[2.5]
Lone parents	[31.5]	68.5	36.7	*
TOTAL POPULATION	60.5	39.5	11.7	1.7
% in bottom quintile**	13.1	26.9	39.6	54.1
GR				
Retired	31.2	68.8	35.6	9.9
Sick	28.9	71.1	36.2	[12.5]
Adults	44.5	55.5	20.6	5.2
Lone parents	[33.7]	66.3	[36.6]	*
TOTAL POPULATION	42.1	57.9	24.7	6.5
% in bottom quintile**	6.8	31.5	44.8	57.7
PT				
Retired	48.7	51.3	27.1	10.0
Sick	46.6	53.4	24.8	9.6
Adults	66.0	34.0	15.0	5.1
Lone parents	64.5	35.5	[22.8]	*
TOTAL POPULATION	62.5	37.5	17.2	6.0
% in bottom quintile**	9.4	36.4	48.3	58.9
UK				
Retired	60.8	39.2	14.8	2.3
Sick	40.9	59.1	29.7	*
Adults	63.0	37.0	14.7	[2.4]
Lone parents	25.6	74.4	38.1	*
TOTAL POPULATION	67.1	32.9	11.8	2.0
% in bottom quintile**	10.2	30.4	40.1	52.2

Notes:
 * Proportions belonging to the bottom quintile according to:
    (a) Housing conditions, (b) Consumer durables, (c) Household necessities
** Proportion of the group belonging to the bottom 20 per cent of the income distribution.

classified as deprived according to none, at least one, at least two and all three criteria – that is, those are in the bottom quintile of the distribution of deprivation scores in the fields of housing conditions, durable goods and household necessities – who are in the bottom quintile of the income distribution.[20] Even though in all countries the majority of the persons who are aged 16 or more and who are in the bottom quintile of the income distribution are classified as deprived according to at least one criterion,[21] the correlation between monetary and non-monetary deprivation looks relatively weak. In Austria only one-third of those who appear in the bottom quintile of all three distributions of aggregate non-monetary welfare indicators are also in the bottom quintile of the income distribution. The corresponding percentages are higher, but not extremely high, in the rest of the countries under examination (between 50 per cent and 60 per cent). Moreover, in all countries the majority of those classified as deprived according to at least two criteria can be found outside the bottom quintile of the income distribution. In most cases, similar results to those reported for the entire population were also obtained for the risk groups.[22] However, due to the fact that in most countries the members of the risk groups were more likely to be located in the bottom quintile of the income distribution, the incidence of simultaneous monetary and non-monetary deprivation in these groups was, usually, higher.

Table 2.7 is similar to Table 2.6. However, this time the approach adopted for the identification of the 'deprived' is less relativistic than in Table 2.6. In Table 2.7 the 'deprived' are classified as those with deprivation scores higher than 60 per cent of the median national deprivation score of the relevant distribution (housing conditions, consumer durables and household necessities). In all other respects, the methodology used in Table 2.7 is similar to that used in Table 2.6. Naturally, in Table 2.7 a higher proportion of the population is classified as suffering from multi-dimensional disadvantage in those countries that register high average deprivation scores in Table 2.4 (Portugal and Greece) than in those with low scores (Austria, Germany and the United Kingdom). Likewise, for the purposes of the identification of the poor in the last line of each panel, the poverty line is set at 60 per cent of the national median equivalent income.

In broad terms the results of Table 2.7 strengthen the results of Table 2.6. It should be noted, though, that in all countries except Portugal, the estimates in the last column of the table (deprived according to all three criteria) cannot be reported in most cases because of the small numbers involved. In all countries, 'Lone parents' and 'Sick' face a substantially higher risk of multi-dimensional disadvantage than the average population member. The relevant risk for the 'Retired' is higher than average in Greece, Portugal and the United Kingdom, whereas 'Young adults' appear to be in

Table 2.7   Comparisons of 'risk groups' in terms of aggregate material non-monetary deprivation indicators (threshold: 60 per cent of the median)

Country per cent risk group	Deprived according to:*			
	No criterion	At least one criterion	At least two criteria	All three criteria
AT				
Retired	85.6	14.4	[2.0]	*
Sick	84.7	[15.3]	*	*
Adults	86.9	13.1	[1.8]	*
Lone parents	84.5	[15.5]	*	*
TOTAL POPULATION	87.6	12.4	1.8	*
% below the poverty line**	14.2	26.6	[40.2]	*
D				
Retired	86.6	13.4	[1.5]	0.0
Sick	73.6	26.4	*	*
Adults	86.3	13.7	[2.3]	*
Lone parents	60.2	39.8	*	0.0
TOTAL POPULATION	87.5	12.5	1.5	*
% below the poverty line**	14.1	31.2	48.4	*
GR				
Retired	53.0	47.0	12.0	1.6
Sick	51.6	48.4	[14.8]	*
Adults	72.7	27.3	4.8	*
Lone parents	[50.5]	[49.5]	*	0.0
TOTAL POPULATION	67.7	32.3	7.2	1.0
% below the poverty line**	12.0	42.1	62.1	69.7
PT				
Retired	55.2	44.8	21.6	6.9
Sick	53.1	46.9	19.3	6.7
Adults	71.9	28.1	11.5	3.8
Lone parents	65.9	34.1	[19.3]	*
TOTAL POPULATION	68.1	31.9	13.2	4.4
% below the poverty line**	13.0	45.8	58.8	65.8
UK				
Retired	80.4	19.6	2.3	0.0
Sick	56.5	43.5	*	0.0
Adults	80.3	19.7	[2.2]	0.0
Lone parents	46.3	53.7	*	0.0
TOTAL POPULATION	82.5	17.5	1.7	0.0
% below the poverty line**	12.9	38.5	48.2	- - -

Notes:
 * Proportions with score below 60 per cent of the median according to:
  (a) Housing amenities, (b) Consumer durables, (c) Household necessities
** Proportion of the group with equivalent income below 60 per cent of the median.

a relatively disadvantaged position in the United Kingdom and, to a lesser extent, Germany. Once again, monetary and non-monetary deprivation do not seem to be very highly correlated. For example, the third column of Table 2.7 shows that, on average, only half of those who are classified as deprived according to two or three of the non-monetary indicators also fall below the income poverty line. However, cross-country differences are considerable; 40.2 per cent in Austria, 48.2 per cent in the United Kingdom, 48.4 per cent in Germany, 58.8 per cent in Portugal and 62.1 per cent in Greece.

SOCIAL TRANSFERS AND POVERTY ALLEVIATION

This section examines the extent to which social transfers contribute to a decline in poverty rates for the four risk groups. Social transfers aim to redistribute income either through various phases or events of an individual's life-cycle or, to a lesser, extent between various population groups. Although in most cases their primary aim is not poverty alleviation, it is one of their most important by-products. As Eardley et al. (1996) point out, the share of social transfers in GDP varies considerably across EU member states and, moreover, in some countries a very significant proportion of these transfers are provided in kind rather than in cash. As noted earlier, information on non-cash transfers is not available in the ECHP. However, the ECHP contains information on five types of social transfers in cash: pensions, sickness and invalidity benefits, family benefits, unemployment benefits and other benefits (consisting mainly of social assistance and cash housing benefits). In all countries, the most important component of social transfers is pensions.[23] However, the most significant cross-country differences with respect to the share of social transfers in household income are observed in the field of non-pension social transfers (Heady et al., 1999). For this reason, apart from the aggregate effect of social transfers on poverty, the corresponding effects that are due to pensions and other social transfers are examined separately.[24]

Table 2.8 presents the total picture in the five countries under examination. The first line of the table reports the proportional decrease in aggregate poverty due to pensions, the second the decrease due to other (non-pension) social transfers and the third the decrease due to all social transfers taken together. The figures in this table should not be interpreted as the proportional increases in poverty in comparison with the poverty rates reported in the first line of Table 2.1 if there were no transfers, but as the proportional decrease in poverty from the level of poverty that would have been encountered if these social transfers did not exist.[25] Starting

Table 2.8 Proportional decline in the aggregate poverty rate due to social transfers in five EU member states

	AT	D	GR	PT	UK
Decline due to pensions alone	52.1	49.3	42.0	29.5	35.8
Decline due to non-pension social transfers alone	36.3	25.6	6.8	14.9	39.5
Decline due to all social transfers	62.3	56.7	43.9	37.8	52.3

from the last line of the table, it can be noted that in all countries social transfers contribute to a very significant decrease in aggregate poverty. Nevertheless, once again, substantial cross-country differences are also evident. Social transfers are most effective in alleviating poverty in the Northern than the Southern EU countries under examination. The proportional decrease in the aggregate poverty rates due to social transfers are between 52.3 per cent and 62.3 per cent in the North (Austria, Germany and the United Kingdom) and 37.8 per cent and 43.9 per cent in the South (Greece and Portugal). In all countries, apart from the United Kingdom, in quantitative terms the contribution of pensions to poverty alleviation is higher than the contribution of all other social transfers combined.[26] Unlike the North, non-pension social transfers do not seem to play a very important role in poverty alleviation in the South, especially in Greece. In the latter case as a result of these transfers the aggregate poverty rate decreased by a mere 6.8 per cent against 25.6–39.5 per cent in the Northern countries.

Table 2.9 is the counterpart of Table 2.8 for the risk groups. However, since the concept of resources used in our analysis is 'equivalent income' – that is the sum of the incomes of all household members divided by the number of 'equivalent adults' in the household – and further, in most cases, social transfers are supposed to support not only their recipients but also the members of their families, it was decided to examine the impact of social transfers on all members of households with at least one member belonging to a risk group.[27] Comparison of the estimates of Table 2.9 with those of Table 2.8 makes apparent some cross-country similarities. In all countries, the proportional decrease in aggregate poverty due to social transfers is higher for the members of households with 'Retired' or 'Sick' persons than for the rest of the population. In contrast, the proportional

Table 2.9 *Proportional decline in the poverty rates of members of households with individuals belonging to a 'risk group' due to social transfers*

Country per cent risk group	Decline due to non-pension social transfers alone	Decline due to pensions alone	Decline due to all social transfers
Retired			
AT	33.8	78.3	80.5
D	22.7	76.9	78.3
GR	76.5	54.7	55.4
PT	11.6	46.5	50.2
UK	41.8	63.2	67.3
Sick or disabled			
AT	47.4	53.7	67.3
D	50.5	46.5	63.9
GR	16.7	40.3	45.3
PT	20.7	22.2	35.9
UK	57.0	13.1	59.1
Young adults			
AT	40.1	40.7	57.2
D	28.4	13.6	36.3
GR	8.2	34.6	38.2
PT	17.9	18.9	32.3
UK	41.4	7.8	45.4
Lone parents			
AT	50.3	21.1	53.7
D	32.0	4.8	33.9
GR	8.9	18.2	26.4
PT	18.2	8.8	25.6
UK	37.6	1.8	38.3

decrease in poverty for the members of households with 'Young adults' or 'Lone parents' is lower than the corresponding decrease for the entire population in all countries under examination. As could be anticipated, the largest proportional decreases in poverty rates after the impact of social transfers is accounted for are recorded in the members of households with 'Retired' persons, whose main source of income is, usually, pensions. Naturally, pensions contribute relatively mildly to the alleviation of poverty among the members of households with 'Young adults' and 'Lone parents', while their impact on members of households with 'Sick' persons is considerable but lower than the corresponding impact on the average population member (except in the case of Austria). In contrast, with few exceptions, in all countries non-pension social transfers result in proportional decreases among members of households with 'Sick', 'Young adults' and 'Lone parents' which are higher than those recorded for the rest of the population.

CONCLUSIONS

The evidence presented in this chapter suggests that a number of similarities and differences can be identified in the five EU member states under examination (Austria, Germany, Greece, Portugal and the United Kingdom) with respect to the relative welfare position of the 'Retired', the 'Sick', the 'Young adults' and the 'Lone parents'. According to most of the indices used, two of these groups – 'Lone parents' and 'Sick' – appear to face a substantially higher risk of poverty, non-monetary material deprivation and multi-dimensional disadvantage than the average population member in all countries under consideration. Further, much of the evidence reported in this chapter suggests that the 'Retired' enjoy a considerably lower standard of living than the rest of the population in the Southern countries (Greece and Portugal) and the United Kingdom. In contrast, with the possible exceptions of Germany and the United Kingdom, the 'Young adults' do not appear to face particularly high risks of poverty and non-monetary material deprivation. Social transfers make a significant contribution to poverty alleviation for all the risk groups – in particular, the 'Retired' and the 'Sick' – especially in the Northern countries (Austria, Germany and the United Kingdom). Naturally, these general results do not imply that there are no specific sub-groups within all the risk groups that may face particularly high or low risks of monetary and/or non-monetary deprivation. This is the subject of the analysis of the next four chapters of this book.

NOTES

1. For example, the studies using the LIS database as well as a number of OECD publications rely on such distributions; see Atkinson et al. (1995).
2. For similar evidence for Portugal, see Rodrigues (1999).
3. Further, all estimates have been derived using the ECHP sample weights, provided by Eurostat.
4. In other words, the denominator in the calculation of equivalent income will be higher (lower).

5. The formula of this family of equivalence scales, W, is:

$$w = (AD + aCH)^b$$

where AD is the number of adults in the household, CH the number of children in the household, a a parameter which shows the relative needs of children ($0 < a < 1$, the higher the value of a the higher the implied needs of a child to those of an adult) and b a parameter that shows the household economies of scale ($0 < b < 1$, the higher the value of b the lower the economies of scale). It should be noted that the 'modified OECD scales' used in the main part of our analysis do not belong to this family of equivalence scales.

6. The formula of the poverty rate, H, is:

$$H = \frac{q}{n}$$

where q is the number of the poor and n the population size.
The formula of the Foster et al. (1984) index, F, is:

$$F = \frac{1}{N} \sum_{i=1}^{n} \left(\frac{z - x_i}{z} \right)^c$$

where z is the poverty line, c a 'poverty-aversion parameter' (the higher its value the higher the weight assigned to the poorest individuals) and x_i a variable that is equal to the equivalent income of the population member if he/she falls below the poverty line and z otherwise. In line with most studies, the value of c used here is equal to 2.
    Further, it should be noted that since the estimates of F are very small in absolute terms, the estimates reported below have been multiplied by 1000. Likewise, in line with most studies, the estimates of H reported below are multiplied by 100 (percentage of the population below the poverty line).

7. Note also that, for exposition purposes, the vertical axes in the graphs of three countries (D, GR, UK) go up to 30 per cent, whereas in the cases of the other two countries (AT and PT) they rise only up to 20 per cent.

8. Note that this share refers to persons aged 16 or more, living in lone-parent headed households. Children aged below 16 are not included in this definition.

9. According to Eurostat's cell size thresholds, numbers in brackets indicate cell sizes of 20–50 cases and an asterisk (*) denotes a – not publishable – cell size of fewer than 20 cases. This rule is followed throughout this book.

10. In order to derive estimates of the poverty rate, H, or the Foster et al. index, F, for particular risk groups, these figures should be multiplied by the corresponding estimates for the entire population of the country under examination that are reported in the first two lines of Table 2.1. In order to calculate their contribution to the aggregate poverty, these figures should be multiplied by the corresponding population shares of the risk groups that are reported in the last four lines of Table 2.1.

11. These results are in line with the results of earlier studies on the status of elderly persons in the EU; see Tsakloglou (1996).

12. Regional effects were also controlled for in all countries apart from Germany whose regional information is suppressed in the user database of the ECHP.

13. These are absolute percentage points in comparison with the estimated poverty risk of the reference group; not proportional changes from estimated poverty risk of the reference group. Taking the example of the first estimate reported in Table 2.3, ceteris paribus, the estimated poverty risk of the reference group in Austria is 16.0 per cent, whereas if we change the individual's employment status from 'Employee' to 'Retired', the estimated poverty risk rises to 24.9 per cent (16.0 + 8.9).

14. It should be noted that even though the results of such an exercise are very informative, their policy implications are not always straightforward, since the estimated effects are derived from a reduced form rather than a structural model. For instance, the fact that somebody is in ill health is likely to reduce his/her employment probability and, hence,

his/her earnings potential. In our regression, this possibility of reduced income may be picked by the fact that many 'Sick' persons are unemployed. However, this reasoning does not invalidate the fact that the poverty risk of the 'Sick' is substantially higher than the national average and, therefore, policies aimed to alleviate poverty among the group's members should be implemented.

15. See, for example, Burchardt et al. (1999) and Nolan et al. (1999).

16. In algebraic terms, the formula for the calculation of each population member's deprivations score, μ_j, is:

$$\mu_j = \frac{\sum_{i=1}^{I} w_i X_{ij}}{\sum_{i=1}^{I} w_i}$$

where I is the total number of amenities/problems for which information is available (15 in the case of housing condition items of the ECHP), w_i is the proportion of the population living in accommodation with housing amenity i (or without reporting problems with item i) and X_{ij} a variable that takes the value of 0 (1) if the dwelling of individual j is (is not) equipped with housing amenity j or does not (does) report problems with item i.

To some extent, the fact that the denominator is higher (lower) in countries where few (many) population members face bad housing conditions and therefore, ceteris paribus, the country's mean deprivation score is lower (higher), facilitates cross-country comparisons using such a deprivation indicator.

17. More specifically the reference person replied that the household 'would like to have (the durable good but cannot afford it'.

18. In this case w_i is set equal to the proportion of the population living in households with durable good i, but X_{ij} takes the value of 1 only if the reference person replied that the lack of the particular good is due to inability to afford it (and not, simply, when the household does not have such a good).

19. Note that these findings are consistent with the findings of earlier studies, which show that as income per capita rises, the average score of the subjective evaluation of well-being of the population rises at a diminishing rate (van Praag et al., 1982).

20. Note that in Tables 2.6 and 2.7 the distribution of 'deprivation scores' is derived from the sample of persons aged 16 or more, whereas the sample of the income distribution consists of all population members. As a result, the proportion of persons aged 16 or more who are located in the bottom quintile of the income distribution may differ from 20 per cent. In fact, in Greece, which is one of the very few EU countries where child poverty is lower than the national average (Immervoll et al. 2000), the share of persons aged 16 or more in the bottom quintile is over 20 per cent (21.1 per cent), whereas the opposite is observed in the rest of the countries under examination (18.3 per cent in Austria, 18.5 per cent in Germany, 19.8 per cent in Portugal and 16.8 per cent in the United Kingdom).

21. The proportion of those aged 16 or more who are simultaneously located in the bottom quintile of the income distribution and classified as deprived according to at least one criterion using the definitions used in this table are 86.3 per cent in Greece, 70.2 per cent in Portugal, 60.1 per cent in Austria, 59.5 per cent in the United Kingdom and 57.3 per cent in Germany.

22. Results available from the authors on request.

23. It should be noted, though, that in the ECHP there is no distinction between private and public pensions and that, for the purposes of our analysis, this distinction is ignored. Since in some countries the share of private pensions in total pension is considerable, the estimates of this section are likely to overestimate the true distributional effects of social transfers. However, this over-estimation is mitigated by the fact that private pensions are more likely to be directed towards the top rather than the bottom of the income distribution.

24. For a detailed analysis of the distributional impact of social transfers in the EU, using the ECHP, see Heady et al. (1999).
25. For example, the first figure of the table, 52.1 per cent, implies that if the poverty line in Austria was kept intact but there were no pensions, the poverty rate would have been 0.332 rather than 0.159. Therefore, the proportional decline in the aggregate poverty rate after the inclusion of pensions is 52.1 per cent (52.1 = 100*(0.332−0.159)/0.332). Further, note that for each country the sum of the estimates reported in the first and the second line of the table is higher than the corresponding estimate reported in third line. This is due to the fact that either pensions or other social transfers alone push many individuals whose income net of social transfers is lower than the level of poverty line above it.
26. Nonetheless, as shown in Heady et al. (1999), this is due to the share of pensions in total income. In almost all EU member states the non-pension social transfers are directed to those close to the bottom end of the income distribution to a substantially larger extent than pensions.
27. Nevertheless, the results for the members of the risk groups only, are virtually indistinguishable from the results reported in Table 2.9.

3. Transitions from youth to adulthood

Sue Middleton

The pathway from dependent child to independent adult in industrialised countries is perhaps better described as a series of transitions that may, or may not, take place sequentially. The European Commission identifies four major transitional events which characterise the change from childhood to adulthood: 'leaving the parental home, finishing school or college, getting a job and forming a couple' (Eurostat, 1997, p. 4). Each of these events might increase the risk of poverty and social exclusion.

In this chapter the impact of these transitional events on young people in our study countries is described. Young people's educational, labour market and family circumstances are first explored, in the context of a comparison of the economic and social policies and programmes which might affect their ability to negotiate successfully the path to adulthood. Finally the extent of poverty and social exclusion among young people is examined and sub-groups of young people particularly at risk are identified. The conclusion considers the implications of these findings for policies targeted on youth transitions.

Each country in our study adopts different ages at which young people are allowed access to the social, economic and citizenship rights that differentiate children from adults. Hence, in order to allow direct comparisons to be made among countries, it was necessary to agree an age range for the analysis. This needed to be sufficiently wide so that the vast majority of those younger than the lower age limit would have few, if any, of the rights and responsibilities associated with adulthood, whilst most of those older than the upper age limit would have entered full adult status. Therefore, for the purposes of this study young people are defined as aged 16 to 29 years. In order to explore the changing nature of young people's lives as they move through this lengthy period of change, in most of what follows young people are further subdivided into three age groups: 16–19 years; 20–24 years; and 25–29 years.

Each country has between approximately one-fifth and one-quarter of its population aged between 16 and 29 years, with Norway having the largest percentage of its population in the transition group and Germany the lowest (Table 3.1). Breaking down the transitional group into those aged 16–19 years, 20–24 years and 25–29 years shows how the population of young people in each country is declining with each successive cohort. All countries have the lowest percentage of young people in the 16–19 year group and, with the exception of Portugal and Norway, the highest percentage aged from 25 to 29 years.

Table 3.1   Young adults in the population (column per cent)

	AT	D	GR	N	PT	UK
16–19 years	6	4	5	7	7	5
20–24 years	9	6	8	10	10	7
25–29 years	11	9	8	10	8	9
Total 16–29 years	26	19	21	27	25	21

Two factors are accepted to be largely responsible for the decrease in the proportion of young people in the population. Women in Europe are starting their families at a later age and having fewer children (see further below). At the same time people are living longer and, therefore, spending longer periods outside of the labour market in retirement (see Chapter 6).

ACHIEVING ECONOMIC INDEPENDENCE

Central to the transition from youth to adulthood is the move from financial dependence on parents to financial independence. One manifestation of a 'successful' transition is the move from full-time education to full-time secure work. The age at which this occurs will inevitably vary according to a range of factors, such as when the individual completes full-time education, the availability of full-time secure jobs for young people and, indeed, the general condition of the labour market within each country. This section describes policies relating to young people's participation in education, training and employment, and uses data from the ECHP to explore if, and to what extent, these policies appear to be impacting on young people's lives as they make the transition from full-time education to the adult labour market.

Education

Education policies

The minimum age at which young people are permitted to leave full-time education increased progressively in each study country throughout the second half of the twentieth century. The minimum school leaving age is now 15 or 16 years, with three further years of compulsory part-time schooling in Germany. It seems that most young people stay at school until this age, despite some evidence from Portugal of continuing, if decreasing, early drop out from compulsory schooling.

Governments have had a dual motive to encourage participation in education and training beyond compulsory schooling. First, longer periods in education and training should promote employment prospects among young people and improve the skill base of the workforce. Second, encouraging more young people to remain in education to a later age should, at least in the short term, reduce levels of youth unemployment.

Participation in education following compulsory schooling is voluntary in all countries with the exception of Germany. Policies to assist young people to remain in education take three forms: first, direct support to educational institutions; second, direct financial support to young people to assist them to remain in education; finally, indirect support to families through the continued provision of family benefits for young people in education.

Governments in all six countries fund second and third level educational institutions. For the third level all universities are public, with the exception of Portugal where private institutions are on the increase. Students in Portugal also have to pay tuition fees and, from September 1999, this has also been the case in the UK. Means-tested assistance with these fees is available in both countries.

Governments also provide some level of assistance to young people with their living costs in all countries except Portugal and Greece. Means-tested grants are available in Austria and Germany and these are supplemented by loans in Germany. Such grants were also available in the UK at the time of the survey but in 1998 were finally replaced by a system of loans. Means tests are generally conducted on the income of parents, so that young people remain dependent on their parents for any shortfall in their income. However, the means test for grants was applied to the young person's income after the age of 21 years in the UK. Loans are means-tested in Norway and Germany but available to any student in the UK. Germany and Austria also condition continued eligibility for assistance on proof of educational progress.

In all countries except Germany and Norway, where grants are also available for high school students, direct assistance is confined to those in third level education. Reforms at the end of 1999 in Germany are intended to provide further encouragement to young people to stay on in education through a range of measures, including increases in the maximum level of financial support for young people and relaxing the conditions of the means test. In the UK a special allowance for young people aged 16 to 19 years from lower income families who remain in full-time education is being piloted.

Finally, all countries except the UK continue to pay the main benefit for children for those who continue in higher education. In Austria and Greece the maximum age is 26 years and in Germany 28 years. In Austria the family allowance can be paid directly to the young person, rather than to the parents, and the young person does not have to be living in the parental home to receive the allowance.

Students are largely excluded from insurance-based benefits because of inadequate contributions records. Countries vary in the extent to which students can supplement their income through social assistance. Students in Germany and the UK, for example, are not entitled to claim social assistance, whereas in Norway they may do so during the two months of the year for which the system of loans and grants does not provide. In Austria entitlement to social assistance is dependent on the income of parents.

In most countries, therefore, remaining in education is accompanied by continued dependence on parents for financial support and, inevitably, a delay in labour market entry and the possibility of financial independence.

Education outcomes

The extent and level of state financial support for young people remaining in education beyond compulsory school leaving age is not accurately reflected in the proportions of young people participating in education. Whilst the relatively generous system of support in Norway is matched by the highest levels of participation in all age groups, Portugal and Greece with the least generous provision have the next highest participation rates for 16–29 year olds and the UK the lowest (Table 3.2). There are at least three possible reasons for this. First, the alternatives to staying in education for young people in Portugal and Greece are perhaps more limited and not as attractive as in other countries. Second, the low figures for the UK, collected in 1994, might fail to reflect fully the massive increases in participation in further and higher education which had taken place only a couple of years previously. It is likely that this expansion will be reflected in increased proportions of 20–29 year olds remaining in education in the UK in subsequent waves of the ECHP.

Finally, at least part of the explanation for the low UK figures must lie

Table 3.2   Participation in education and training by age and gender (cell per cent)

	16–19 years	20–24 years	25–29 years	All 16–29 years	Men 16–29 years	Women 16–29 years
Austria	38	21	(7)	19	19	21
Germany	45	21	13	22	27	24
Greece	68	27	(4)	28	26	24
Norway	79	37	15	39	38	39
Portugal	56	33	7	31	23	32
UK	38	9	*	12	11	12

in the exclusion from the ECHP of people living in residential establishments. Many UK students in universities live in such accommodation and the ECHP therefore underestimates the percentage of UK young people in third level education. These figures, therefore, should be treated with some caution.

With the exception of Germany and Greece, it seems that more women than men were in education and training in 1994. This reflects the culmination of a trend towards higher participation rates in education by young women which has been described elsewhere (Eurostat, 1997).

Another way of measuring whether policies to improve educational standards are succeeding is to compare levels of educational achievement among younger people in the population with those for the population as a whole (Table 3.3). If policies are succeeding then the

Table 3.3   Highest educational level achieved (cell per cent)

	First Level Secondary		Second Level Secondary		Third Level	
	16–29 years	All adults	16–29 years	All adults	16–29 years	All adults
AT	27	35	68	60	5	6
D	36	33	56	48	8	19
GR	31	59	49	25	20	16
PT	69	83	27	12	4	5
UK	41	48	43	32	15	20

Notes: Figures for Norway not available.

proportion of young people with the lowest level of educational achievement (first level secondary) would be lower than for adults as a whole.
Conversely, the proportions of young people achieving higher qualifications (second level secondary and third level) would be higher than for
adults as a whole. Table 3.3 suggests that policies to improve educational
standards are, in general, having the desired effect. With the exception
of Germany, fewer young people have completed only first level secondary education than all adults, and in all countries more young people
have completed second level secondary education than in the whole population. The figures for third level education are less easy to interpret,
since only in Greece have larger percentages of young people achieved
third level education qualifications than in the population at large. The
most likely explanation is that many young people were still in third level
education at the time of interview, although this does not explain the
Greek figures.

Despite these general improvements in educational standards *within*
countries, the gaps *between* countries remain large. In all countries at least
one quarter of young people have completed only first level education but
in Portugal this is so for more than two-thirds. However, the situation is
improving rapidly. Greece can be seen to have made the largest improvements with almost 50 per cent fewer young people completing only first
level education than adults as a whole. In Greece and Portugal the proportion of young people who have completed second level secondary education is around twice as high as for adults in general.

It seems that policies designed to improve educational standards are succeeding in these countries. Further analysis (not reported here) suggests
that much of this success is the result of increased participation rates by
young women in second and third level education. However, participation
rates seem to be unconnected to the generosity of financial support that
governments extend to young people who stay on in education.

Employment

The inevitable result of longer periods spent in education is that entry to
the labour market will, on average, take place later. There is of course no
guarantee that (suitable) jobs will be available for young people at the point
at which they finally complete their education and wish to move into the
labour market. All countries provide a range of measures for those young
people who have completed their education and who are unable to find
work. Most operate a mixture of supply- and demand-side policies aimed
at improving the qualifications of young people for work and encouraging
employers to take them on.

Supply-Side Policies

All countries have vocationally orientated training schemes and pro-grammes that are specifically targeted on assisting young people to make the transition into the labour market. In Germany, Austria and the UK, governments have been forced to become more pro-active in the provision of vocational education and training as the availability of traditional craft and trade apprenticeships has decreased. The declining importance of the manufacturing industry, economic globalisation and competition, and recession have made companies reluctant to meet the costs of training. Germany has introduced a raft of new measures to provide apprenticeships since 1994, particularly in the former East Germany, and Austria has initi-ated 23 new apprenticeship programmes since 1997. In the UK new, voca-tionally orientated qualifications have been introduced as an alternative to traditional academic qualifications. The 'New Deal' policies, introduced since 1997 and aimed at reducing unemployment among specific target groups, including young people, involve provision for education and train-ing for all young people who participate.

Portugal and Greece also provide training programmes that are specifi-cally targeted on young unemployed people. Greece, along with Norway and Germany, is focusing on making education more relevant to the needs of the economy. In Portugal a series of relatively recent training initiatives are designed to cater for various groups of the unemployed, with differing age ranges and levels of qualification. The programmes contain both theor-etical and practical elements, and are specifically aimed at assisting integra-tion in the labour market. However, the effects of these policies are unlikely to be seen in the survey data for some years.

In addition to these educational 'carrots', most countries have a finan-cial 'stick' to encourage unemployed young people into work, education or training. In most countries receipt of social assistance is dependent on accepting some form of work, education or training. The introduc-tion of 'workfare' in Norway in 1993 was specifically aimed at reducing the numbers of young social assistance claimants. In the UK single young people under the age of 25 years receive lower rates of benefit/social assistance when unemployed than other groups. Further, under the 'New Deal' policies that commenced in 1998, unemployment on benefit is not an option for almost all young people after the first six months.

Demand-Side Policies
Most countries also operate a range of demand-side measures to increase labour market demand for young people. In summary these include:

1. the provision of subsidies to employers who take on young unemployed people or who provide a 'first job' (Greece, Norway, Portugal, UK);
2. providing specially created jobs for young people in the public sector (Germany, Norway);
3. making it generally easier and cheaper for employers to hire workers (Germany, UK); and
4. removing minimum wage restrictions or having a lower minimum wage for young people (UK).

Employment outcomes
It seems that the extensive range of demand and supply side measures described above are meeting with, at best, limited success. On the positive side, levels of employment increase with age for the three younger age groups, and are higher for young people as a whole than for all adults in four of the six countries (Table 3.4). Greece, with the least developed programmes for labour market insertion, has the lowest levels of employment for each age group and Austria the highest. Only a little over two-fifths of young people in Greece are in employment compared with well over two-thirds in Austria.

Table 3.4   Employment and unemployment (cell per cent)

	AT	D	GR	N	PT	UK
Employed:						
16–19 years	54	46	13	12	34	47
19–24 years	67	63	40	42	52	71
24–29 years	82	73	63	71	79	75
All young people	70	64	42	46	56	67
All adults	56	53	42	46	55	55
Unemployed:						
16–19 years	*	(6)	12	2	5	(12)
19–24 years	(3)	(7)	21	10	9	11
24–29 years	*	5	15	8	7	5
All young people	3	(6)	16	7	7	(8)
All adults	3	5	6	7	5	4

However, 'employment' can cover a range of activity states, each of which will provide more or less security and financial reward. What young people are actually doing when describing their main activity as 'employment' can be seen to differ significantly from country to country, largely according to the level and types of supply-side programmes provided (Table 3.5). Whilst nine out of ten young people who are employed in Norway and the UK are in paid employment, only two-thirds are in paid work in Greece and three-quarters in Germany. The remaining young people in Greece are involved in self-employment or unpaid family work, whereas German young people are in paid apprenticeships under their more advanced supply-side measures. In fact, more than four-fifths of German-employed 16–19 year olds are in a paid apprenticeship or employment training and almost one half of those in Austria (figures not shown). Levels are very much lower in each of the other countries where programmes are less well developed, non-existent or, as in Norway, where much higher percentages of young people are still in education.

Table 3.5   Type of employment activity: young people aged 16–29 years (column per cent)

	AT	D	GR	N	PT	UK
Paid employment	84	76	66	91	86	90
Paid apprenticeship	2	18	*	5	*	*
Employment training	(8)		*	0	*	(1)
Self-employment	4	7	15	4	7	7
Unpaid family work	(2)		17	0	5	*

This pattern seems to be reflected in levels of unemployment among young people, which are particularly disturbing in Greece and the UK. Greek young people are two-and-a-half times more likely to be unemployed than all adults, and UK young people twice as likely (Table 3.4). Unemployment is particularly prevalent in the two youngest age groups in the UK and in the 19–24 year age group in Greece. In the other four countries youth unemployment rates are the same, or only very slightly higher, for young people as for all adults.

Further analysis has shown that, with the exception of the UK, young women are more likely to be unemployed than young men (figures not shown). In Greece and Norway young women are more than one-and-a-half times more likely to be unemployed than young men. In the UK young men are more than three times more likely to be unemployed than young women.

Measuring unemployment only at the time of interview underestimates the proportions of the adult population who have experienced unemployment at some time in their working lives. It also tells us nothing about the length of time for which people were unemployed. Examining youth unemployment from these perspectives tells a somewhat different, and more worrying, tale (Table 3.6). Young people in all countries were much more likely to have experienced unemployment in the five years before 1994 than were adults as a whole. However, in general young people in those countries with well-established supply-side policies (Germany and Austria) seemed to do less badly when compared with all adults, although Portugal had similar figures to Austria and Germany. In Greece and Norway young people were two-and-a-half times more likely to have experienced unemployment in the previous five years than adults as a whole. The Norwegian policy response of keeping young people in education does not seem to have helped to keep youth unemployment low. For young people in the UK, facing generally high levels of unemployment and relatively weak supply-side measures, the likelihood of experiencing unemployment was very high.

Table 3.6   *Experience of unemployment and long-term unemployment (cell per cent)*

	AT	D	GR	N	PT	UK
Unemployed in last five years:						
20–29 years	29	29	43	21	29	40
All adults	16	18	17	8	17	22
Unemployed for longer than one year in last five years:						
20–29 years	(14)	25	61	13	43	31
All adults	26	40	56	34	50	37

On a more positive note, in general young people were less likely to have experienced *long-term* unemployment in the previous five years than adults as a whole. Again this was particularly so in Austria and Germany with the best developed supply-side programmes, but was also the case in Norway. However, long-term unemployment rates for young people were not much lower than for all adults in Portugal and the UK, and were higher for young people in Greece.

LEAVING PARENTS AND MAKING NEW FAMILIES

For most people the transition from dependent child to independent adult involves leaving the parental home and setting up new independent households, either alone, with a partner and, in either state, sometimes with children. However, unlike the plethora of schemes and programmes which are available in most countries to assist young people in making the transition from education to the labour market, the role of governments in assisting young people making the transition to independent living is generally a minor one. Family solidarity is strongly promoted throughout Europe, with young people being seen as the responsibility of their parents. It is assumed that young people will remain in the parental home and, as a result, in most countries there is little independent assistance for young people in their own right.

As mentioned above, financial provision to assist parents bringing up children is made in all six countries and it is common for this to be paid until the child is deemed to be independent, usually between the ages of 16 and 18 years. In all countries except the UK and Norway, benefits can be extended when the child is unemployed or continuing in education but remain payable to the parent. Only in Austria have some young people – students – been entitled to receive the family allowance directly and, as described earlier, this right has been curtailed.

Eligibility of young people for other financial benefits is also restricted in most countries. Young people are unlikely to have the necessary contribution records to qualify for insurance-based benefits and are forced to depend on the less generous means-tested subsidiary benefit systems. Young people's entitlement to this is either restricted (the UK), conditional on some form of 'workfare' arrangements (UK, Norway, Germany, Austria), or assessed on the basis of parents' income (Austria).

Access to housing and/or benefits to assist with housing costs is also restricted. In Greece young people are ineligible for housing benefit and in the UK entitlement is severely restricted for those under 25 years of age. Shortages in social housing provision for young people are reported in Norway and single young people in the UK are usually ineligible for social housing.

Young People's Households and Families

Most young people between the ages of 16 and 19 years continue to live with their parents in each country (Figure 3.1). This is particularly so in Austria and Portugal, where around nine out of ten 16–19 year olds live with their parents, and much less so in Norway where the rate falls to approximately three-quarters. The proportion of young people remaining in the family home then falls for each of the successive age cohorts in each country but to varying degrees. More than two-fifths of Greek (43 per cent) and Portuguese (42 per cent) 25–29 year olds are still living with their parents, compared with only 10 per cent of Norwegian and 14 per cent of UK young people.

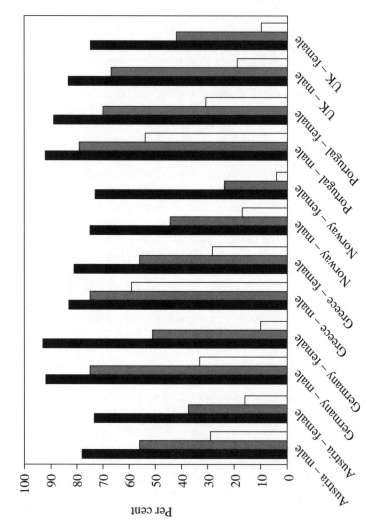

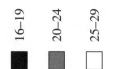

16–19

20–24

25–29

Figure 3.1   Young people living with parents

However, the most striking feature of Figure 3.1 is the difference between young men and young women. For each country and in each age group, with the exception of German 16–19 year olds, fewer young women than young men are living in the parental home. These differences are relatively small for the youngest age cohort but rapidly increase, so that for 25–29 year olds four times more Norwegian men than Norwegian women are living with their parents, three times more German men than women and twice as many UK men. It seems, therefore, that these data confirm findings from previous studies suggesting that whilst young people are staying with their parents for longer, this is particularly so for young men.

The destinations of young men and women when they do leave their parents also show major differences. Figure 3.2 compares the proportions of young people living alone or in new families either with a partner and no children, with a partner and children or as a single parent (the 16–19 year group has been omitted since so few are not living with parents).

It seems that far more young women than young men form new relationships between the ages of 20 and 29 years. Women in each country and in both age groups are more likely than men to have acquired a partner and/or children. Differences between young men and young women in the proportions living alone are small in each country. These two findings, together with the data shown in Figure 3.1, suggest that young men are still living at home with their parents when young women of the same age are forming new relationships. However, some differences between the countries can be seen. It seems that very few young people of either sex in Portugal and Greece live alone and much smaller percentages in Portugal form new relationships than in the other countries. Greece combines low rates of living alone with rates of new family formation similar to Austria which, in turn, has relatively large percentages of young people living alone. In contrast, much larger numbers of Norwegian young people in both age groups and of both genders live alone, but Norway also has high rates of new family formation, similar to those in the UK. However, the UK does not combine these high rates with large percentages of young people living alone.

Further differences can be seen in the extent to which young people have already formed relationships, both between young men and young women and among young people in different countries (Figure 3.3). Greece and Portugal have the lowest proportions of young people who have formed new relationships, Norway and the UK the highest with Germany and Austria in between.

In contrast to the overall picture, gender differences follow a similar pattern in each country. Young women are more likely to be married than young men, with the difference being particularly large in Greece and Portugal.

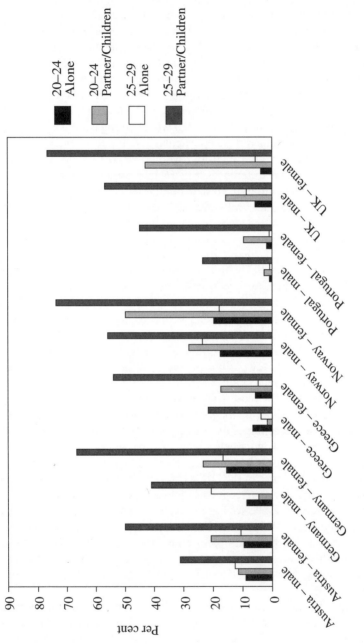

■	20–24 Alone
▨	20–24 Partner/Children
□	25–29 Alone
▨	25–29 Partner/Children

Figure 3.2   Young people living alone and in new relationships

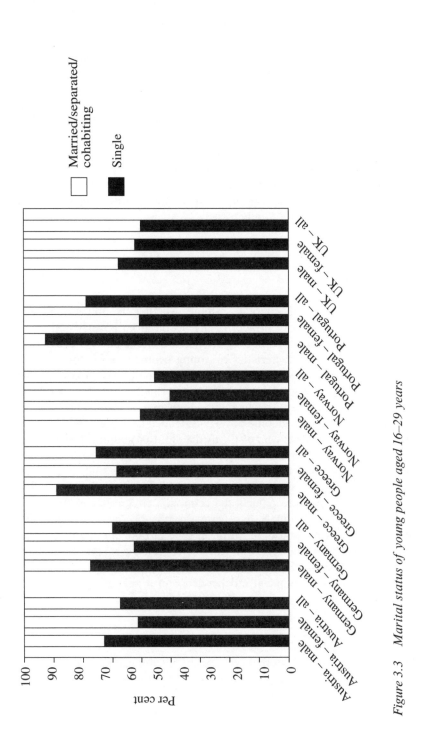

Figure 3.3   Marital status of young people aged 16–29 years

The conclusion from this analysis of young people's living arrangements seems to be that extended periods spent in the family home and later marriage seem to be a male phenomenon. Young women are less likely to live at home, more likely to form new relationships, are less likely to be single and more likely to be married than young men in the same age group. This is so in all our study countries, although the extent of this pattern varies, with young people in Greece and Portugal being more likely still to be living with parents and to move directly from home into marriage. It seems that social policies that are either designed to ensure or assume that young people will remain the responsibility of their parents are having the desired effect, but particularly for young men.

YOUNG PEOPLE, POVERTY AND SOCIAL EXCLUSION

The final section of this chapter examines whether the policies and programmes described above protect young people from poverty and social exclusion. First, young people's experience of income poverty is explored and the particular characteristics of young people in each country that seem to be associated with income poverty are described. Second, other measures of deprivation and social exclusion available from the ECHP are considered and the extent to which these overlap with income poverty.

As in other chapters, income poverty is defined as living in a household with income below 60 per cent of the median for that country. This has particular implications for measuring poverty among young people. It was shown earlier in this chapter that many young people, and particularly those in the youngest age group, are living at home with their parents. The income poverty measure reflects the economic circumstances of households rather than individuals. In other words, the income poverty measure describes the circumstances of young people in poor households, rather than necessarily of young people themselves. However, this reflects the essence of the economic transition to adulthood – from financial dependence on parents to financial independence in a new household and/or family.

Income Poverty

At first sight it might seem that poverty among young people is not a particular issue for most of our study countries. With the exception of Norway, poverty rates are either lower than for adults as a whole or only marginally higher (Table 3.7).

Table 3.7   Income poverty among young people (cell per cent)

	AT	D	GR	N	PT	UK
16–19 years	18	23	22	14	20	18
20–24 years	15	21	18	28	17	14
25–29 years	14	17	13	12	14	15
All young people	15	20	17	19	17	15
All adults	17	18	21	12	24	21

The similarity in poverty rates between all adults and young people might suggest that there is no need for anti-poverty policies particularly targeted at young people who will benefit from strategies aimed at reducing poverty in the population as a whole. Although poverty for young people is most prevalent among the youngest age group in all countries, again with the exception of Norway, this could be a reflection of higher poverty rates among households with children rather than a particular characteristic of this younger age group.

However further investigation, using logistic regression models to identify characteristics particularly associated with poverty, suggests a slightly more complex picture.[1] Table 3.8 lists the socio-economic characteristics that are significantly more or less likely to be associated with poverty among young people in each country. In other words, it shows the circumstances that are most likely to lead to poverty for young people and those which are most likely to protect young people from poverty. Characteristics in italics are shared by the adult population as a whole. In other words, having such a characteristic is significantly more likely to be associated with poverty for the adult population as a whole – it is not simply related to young people. Policies to address poverty caused or prevented by these characteristics need to be aimed at the adult population in general. Those characteristics not in italics are significantly associated with poverty only for young people and policy interventions might usefully be targeted accordingly.[2] The reference group for each characteristic is shown in parenthesis.

It seems that higher levels of poverty are most closely associated with personal and household circumstances in Austria and Germany, whereas in Greece they are the result of low educational qualifications and labour market status. Analysis for Portugal and the UK shows a mixture of characteristics that are likely to cause poverty, with no less than six characteristics in the UK being significantly associated with an increased risk of poverty.

In terms of characteristics that protect young people from poverty, in all

Table 3.8   Factors that prevent or increase poverty among young people

	Factors that increase poverty	Factors that decrease poverty
AT	Female (male) *Living alone* (with both parents)	Aged 20–29 years (aged 16–19 years)
D	Lone parent (living with both parents) *Living alone* (with both parents)	Aged 20–29 years (aged 16–19 years)
GR	*Less than secondary education (second stage secondary)* *In education (in employment)* *Unemployed (in employment)* *Caring for home and family (in employment)*	Aged 25–29 years (aged 16–19 years) *Couple with children (with both parents)* *Couple without children (with both parents)*
PT	Living with a lone parent (with both parents) *Unemployed (in employment)* *Care of home and family (in employment)*	Aged 20–29 years (aged 16–19 years)
UK	Living with a lone parent (with both parents) Living alone (with both parents) Lone parent (with both parents) *Less than secondary stage secondary education* *Unemployed (in employment)* *Care of home and family (in employment)*	Aged 20–29 years (aged 16–19 years) *Cohabiting (married)* *Third stage education (second stage secondary)*

Note: Data for Norway not available

countries poverty is particularly associated with the younger end of our age range. Young people aged 20–24 years are significantly less likely to be poor than those aged 16–19 years in four of the six countries and those aged 25–29 years are less likely to be poor in all countries. There are no other family or labour market characteristics that are significant in protecting young people from poverty.

However, this does not mean that poverty is something that young people will grow out of, along with acne and adolescent tantrums. In each country except Greece there are characteristics that are significantly more likely to be associated with increased levels of poverty among young people that do not result in significantly higher levels of poverty for adults as a whole. In Austria, for example, simply being young and female increases the risk of poverty, whereas in Germany and the UK being a young lone parent, most of whom are women, carries a risk of poverty ten times greater than being young and married. In Portugal and the UK living with your own, lone parent increases the chances of being poor, as does living alone in the UK.

The remaining characteristics that encourage or prevent poverty are shared by all adults. All the factors that are significantly associated with youth poverty in Greece are shared by adults as a whole, that is, factors associated with educational achievement and the labour market.

Another way of assessing the effectiveness of state intervention in reducing poverty is to measure the extent to which household poverty would increase if pensions and other social transfers, mainly social assistance, were withdrawn from household income. Table 3.9 shows the extent to which the percentage of poor households with young people would increase if pensions, social transfers and private transfers were removed from household income and compares this with the impact of pensions and social transfers on poverty among all adults.

The combination of pensions and other social transfers plays a much smaller role in preventing poverty among young people than among all adults in each country. This is largely because of the much smaller percentage contribution of pensions to the incomes of households with young people. However, pensions and social transfers in Austria combine to reduce poverty among young people by 19 per cent, much more than in the three other countries for which full data are available. In Greece pensions

Table 3.9   *The role of transfers in preventing poverty among households with young people (cell per cent)*

	AT	D[1]	GR	PT	UK
Young People:					
Pensions	9	2	8	4	2
Other social transfers	10	–	2	4	10
All Adults:					
Pensions	21	22	18	12	15
Other social transfers	8	–	1	5	13

Notes:
Table reads 'additional percentage of young people who would be in poverty if the social transfer/pension were removed from the household'.
Data for Norway not available.
1. Pension data only is available for Germany.

reduce poverty by four times as much as social transfers, whereas in the UK social transfers account for five times the reduction in poverty compared with pensions.

Social transfers reduce poverty by similar amounts for young people and all households in each country but at very different levels. Ten per cent more young people would be income poor if social transfers were withdrawn in Austria and the UK, compared with only 2 per cent in Greece and 4 per cent in Portugal. This is because of the very limited availability of social transfers generally in Portugal and Greece and the much wider dependence on social transfers in Austria and the UK. However, whereas in the UK a smaller proportion of young people are being kept out of poverty by social transfers than adults as a whole, in Austria more young people are apparently dependent on social transfers than among the adult population in general.

Material Deprivation and Income Poverty

Income poverty is only one of a range of poverty measures. Our analysis explored four other measures of poverty in relation to young people. The first asks whether young people are deprived of a list of six household amenities; the second examines deprivation of seven consumer durables; the third describes nine items associated with living in poor housing and/or a poor neighbourhood; and, finally, going without a list of seven household and personal necessities because of lack of money. Scores on each item within these measures were combined to give an overall 'deprivation' score relative to the population as a whole.[3] In other words, the data in Table 3.10 should not be taken to mean that, for example, Greek young people are less likely to be deprived of household amenities than young people in other countries. Rather the measure is relative and has already taken account of the much higher overall levels of deprivation in some countries, particularly Greece and Portugal.

In general only very small differences emerge in each country between material deprivation among young people and the adult population as a whole (Table 3.10). The most likely explanation for this is that, as shown above, a large proportion of young people in each country continue to live with their parents. They are therefore sharing the living standards of their parents and, hence, show similar patterns of material deprivation.[4] However, there are one or two exceptions to this. First, young people in each country except Portugal are more likely to be deprived than adults in general. Second, German young people are much more likely than adults as a whole to live in households that are deprived of basic amenities.

It was then possible to examine the proportions of young people who are 'poor' on each measure according to whether or not they are also income-

Table 3.10 Young people and material deprivation (cell per cent)

	AT		D		GR		PT		UK	
	Young people	All adults	Young people	All adults	Young people	All adults	Young people	All adults	Young people	All adults
Household amenities	16	16	29	21	14	16	21	21	16	15
Consumer durables	25	20	29	23	22	20	19	21	23	17
Housing/neighbourhood	19	20	17	18	20	20	21	21	17	19
Household and personal necessities	19	19	20	18	18	23	20	22	19	18

Note: Data for Norway not available.

Table 3.11 Material deprivation and income poverty among young people (cell per cent)

	AT		D		GR		PT		UK	
Deprived of:	Poor	Non-poor	Poor	Non-poor	Poor	Non-poor	Poor	Non-poor	Poor	Non-poor
Household amenities	23	13	37	22	21	11	35	14	27	15
Consumer durables	32	24	36	27	38	19	46	13	55	17
Housing/ neighbourhood	26	22	25	21	22	20	23	21	34	23
Household and personal necessities	24	19	34	17	31	14	38	16	45	14

Note: Data for Norway not available.

poor. In other words, Table 3.11 explores the degree of overlap between these measures of material deprivation and income poverty. Whilst income poor young people are more likely to be deprived on each measure of material deprivation than non-poor young people (as are adults as a whole), the extent of the overlap is not large. Income-poor young people are only slightly more likely to live in poor quality housing than non-income-poor young people, suggesting that housing quality is not necessarily associated with income. The differences for the other measures are larger, particularly for consumer durables in Portugal and the UK where income-poor young people are more than three times more likely to be deprived of consumer durables than non-income-poor young people.

Social Relations and Income Poverty

One approach to measuring social exclusion is to explore the extent to which people are deprived of contacts with family and friends. The ECHP asks individuals about their membership of clubs and organisations, contacts with neighbours and meetings with friends and/or relatives (Table 3.12).

Greek and Portuguese young people are far less likely to belong to clubs than young people in other countries but are more likely to have contact with neighbours. This parallels the experience of adults as a whole in these countries and probably reflects the relative absence of such organisations.

Table 3.12   Young people and social relationships (cell per cent)

| | AT | | D | | GR | | PT | | UK | |
	Young people	All adults	Young people	All adults	Young people	All adults	Young people	All adults	Young people	All adults
Not a member of club/organisation	54	58	48	50	91	91	85	85	58	54
Talks to neighbours less than once or twice a month	31	21	29	17	7	6	14	12	23	16
Meets friends/relatives less than once or twice a month	15	31	11	28	6	11	22	29	8	16

Notes: Data for Norway not available.

Poverty and social exclusion in Europe

*Table 3.13   Social relations and income poverty: young people
(cell per cent)*

	AT		D		GR		PT		UK	
	Poor	Non-poor	Poor	Non-poor	Poor	Non-poor	Poor	Non-poor	Poor	Non-poor
Not a member of a club/organisation										
Young people	63	53	53	47	93	90	88	85	71	55
All adults	63	56	57	48	96	90	92	82	64	52
Talks to neighbours less than once or twice a month										
Young people	42	29	32	29	5	7	12	14	18	24
All adults	24	21	19	17	4	6	8	13	13	17
Meets friends/relatives less than once or twice a month										
Young people	17	15	13	11	6	7	27	21	10	8
All adults	33	31	31	27	13	11	33	27	15	16

Notes: Data for Norway not available.

In the remaining three countries approximately half of young people belong to clubs, again similar to the levels of membership found among all adults. Over one-fifth of young people talk to their neighbours less than once or twice a month and this level of contact is lower than for adults as a whole.

A different pattern emerges for contacts with friends and/or relatives. Whilst young people in each country, with the exception of Portugal, are at least twice as likely to have such contacts than are all adults, the extent varies among countries. Contact is highest in Greece and the UK and lowest in Portugal where more than one in five young people meet friends and/or relatives less than once a month.

The patterns of overlap between income poverty and this measure of social exclusion are complex (Table 3.13). First, young people in each country show similar patterns of membership of clubs and other organisations to adults, with the income-poor groups being less likely to be members than the non-poor. This is presumably associated with the costs of membership which will stretch the limited resources of the young and adult poor equally. It might be anticipated that, given the association between income poverty and labour market inactivity, income-poor people would have more time for contacts with neighbours and friends and relatives than non-poor people. In fact the picture is more complex. Poor young people are less likely to have regular contacts with neighbours than the non-poor in

Austria and Germany but are more likely to do so in the remaining three countries. Differences between poor and non-poor in levels of contact with friends and relatives are small, with slightly more non-poor young people (and adults) having contacts with friends and family than the poor groups in each country except Greece. However, both poor and non-poor young people in each country are more likely to have such regular contacts than are adults in general.

CONCLUSION

Unlike the other life transitions and risks that are described in this book, the transition from youth to adulthood is characterised by a series of transitions which may take place simultaneously, but more often occur sequentially. Young people complete their education, enter the labour market, achieve financial autonomy and form new households and families, as well as acquiring other rights and obligations of adult citizenship such as military service, voting and criminal liability.

The transition to adulthood is a much more complex experience for European young people today than it was for their parents. Young people are spending longer in education and entering the labour market later. This is encouraging if secure employment is associated with educational achievement. However, many countries are also witnessing high levels of unemployment and, even in countries where unemployment is generally low, youth unemployment is much higher than the average.

It is debatable whether the encouragement of young people to remain in education is a response to labour market problems, or arises from a more long-term concern to upgrade labour force skills in an increasingly competitive and global market place. If a response to youth unemployment, then continued education would appear not to have been entirely successful. Whilst educational participation has increased, youth unemployment remains a problem.

At the same time, policies to encourage education have been the victims of their own success. Governments are now seeking to contain the costs of providing extended education by restricting financial support for students. It is too soon to assess the impact of such retrenchment on future education patterns, but it is clear that in some countries acquiring third level educational qualifications will become significantly more expensive.

Policies to assist young people to leave home and form new households and families are severely limited. Governments continue to assert the responsibility of parents to support their children until they are fully-fledged and able to support themselves financially. Financial autonomy in terms of access to social security and associated benefits is severely restricted in our study countries and, again, entitlement is largely through parents. As a result many young people in each country continue to live at home with their parents until well into their twenties. However, the age at which young people leave the parental home and form new households and families is gender differentiated, with young women in all countries making this transition at an earlier age than young men. Young men stay with their parents longer and form new relationships at a later age than young women. This pattern must at least be partly a response to longer periods spent in education and the inability to obtain secure employment in the labour market.

The outcomes of these findings for poverty among young people vary from country to country. Although, in general, poverty rates among young people are lower than for adults as a whole, specific sub-groups of young people in each country suffer disproportionately from income poverty and policies need to be tailored accordingly. General policies to reduce unemployment are likely to have a positive effect on poverty among young people in Greece, Portugal and the UK. In contrast the more active and extensive supply-side measures that already exist to assist young people into the labour market in Austria and Germany seem to be protecting young people from poverty. In these countries attention needs to be given to the circumstances of young people living alone. The level of attention being given by policy makers in the UK to lone parents would seem to be justified, and needs to be considered in Germany (see further Chapter 4).

Policy attention needs to be focused on young people who are living alone in Austria, Germany and the UK. Whilst encouraging young people to remain at home with their parents will help to protect them from poverty, the plight of those young people who do not or cannot live with their parents should not be ignored.

NOTES

1. Significant at the 0.05 level.
2. A detailed description of how the deprivation scores have been constructed can be found in Chapter 2.
3. Further analysis to test this explanation is not possible because numbers in sub-groups are too small.

4. Lone parenthood*

Jane Millar

The rise in lone parenthood is probably one of the most visible outcomes of changing patterns of family formation and dissolution in western countries and such families have increasingly become the subject of political, policy and research interest at both national and supra-national level. Lone parenthood is a family status, describing a particular family structure – one parent living with his or her children and without a partner – and much attention has been focused on how the situation of lone-parent families compares with that of two-parent families. This research has clearly shown the very high risk of income poverty faced by lone parents in many countries and the importance of employment and family benefits in reducing these poverty risks (for example Hobson, 1994; Bradshaw et al., 1996; Christopher et al., 2001). Lone parents are least likely to be poor in countries where their employment rates are high and where family benefits and transfers are most generous, and vice versa (Millar, 1996; Kilkey and Bradshaw, 1999).

However, lone parenthood is much more than just a family status. Spending time as a lone parent is also part of the wider life course of partnership and parenthood, in which a spell living as a lone parent is an increasingly common experience for many people. Examining lone parenthood as a life-course transition focuses attention on the different ways in which people become lone parents and the impact this has on their current situation. Of course, this is not a life-course transition that is experienced by everyone in society and, in particular, women are much more likely than men to spend time as a lone parent. Women everywhere make up the vast majority – 80–90 per cent – of this family type. Thus, lone parents are a key group for an analysis of the relationship between poverty and gender (Millar, 1996; Lewis, 1997). The situation of lone mothers reflects the situation of women more generally and cross-national comparisons of lone parenthood also cast light on wider issues of gender inequality in different countries.

* This chapter draws in part on the project working paper 'Prevalence, provision and policy debates' written by Sue Middleton and Rebecca Warton, 1998.

Lone parenthood is also rather different from the other transitions examined for this project. Transitions to adulthood, retirement and, to a lesser extent, ill health or disability are largely unavoidable, inevitable and irreversible. In contrast, the experience of lone parenthood is unpredictable, affects a relatively small number of families and, by definition, is time limited. Children grow up, lone parents repartner. Yet policies in most countries in our study assume that the condition is static and unchanging.

Concerns about the growth in the numbers of families with children headed by single adults, usually women, have surfaced in some, but by no means all, countries of the European Union during the 1990s. As noted above, lone parenthood is one manifestation of the rapidly changing demography of family and working life in Europe. In general, Europeans are older when they get married, have their children later and have fewer of them than in earlier years. They are more likely to cohabit, rather than marry, and less likely to stay with the same partner for life. Women are more likely to be active in the labour market, both before and after childbirth. These trends are more apparent in some countries than in others, but all European countries are experiencing significant changes in patterns of family formation and dissolution. Yet the welfare policies of most countries are predicated on traditional assumptions about the male as breadwinner and the woman as housekeeper in the context of a network of local family support. Policies and systems that were designed in an era of greater family solidarity and stability struggle to adapt to the challenges of changing family structures and women's roles.

From a gendered perspective, these six countries provide a range of different approaches to welfare provision. Austria, Germany and the UK have been described as 'male breadwinner' states; countries where the focus of policy has been to support men in the labour market as breadwinners and women at home as carer-dependants (Lewis, 1997). Norway has traditionally been closer to this breadwinner model than other Scandinavian countries (Leira, 1992) but has increasingly shifted to supporting a 'dual breadwinner' model (Skevik, 1999). Greece and Portugal represent countries where much greater reliance is placed upon family support and where the obligations of family members towards each other are an important element in the welfare package (Millar and Warman, 1996).

The aim of this chapter is to compare the situations of lone-parent families in these six countries. There are three main sections. The first considers how to define lone parenthood and argues for a wider definition than is usually adopted for cross-national studies. The second section considers the issue of employment. Expectations about employment vary quite substantially across different countries, with some countries basing policy on the assumption that lone parents should be at home caring for children while others take the opposite view. Between these extremes there is a great deal of policy ambivalence and the issue of lone parents' labour market participation is increasingly becoming a key policy issue in many countries (Millar and Rowlingson, 2001). The final section of the chapter examines poverty and deprivation, comparing lone parents with other families with children. As noted above, it is known from previous studies that lone parents, and particularly lone mothers, are among the poorest section of the population. The ECHP data allow exploration in a little more depth of the consequences of this for living standards and social isolation.

LONE PARENTHOOD: INCIDENCE AND CHARACTERISTICS

As with the other transitions under investigation, differences in the definition of lone parenthood make cross-national statistical comparisons difficult. Most countries define lone parenthood according two main criteria – not living with a partner and age of children – but there are variations in the way these are used (Roll, 1992; Millar, 1994). For example, until recently Norway has included cohabiting couples where the man is not the father of the children in counts of lone-parent families; other countries specifically exclude such couples. Age limits for children often vary. Austria, for example, limits the definition of lone parenthood to families where the youngest child is under 15 years old, whereas the UK age limit is under 16 years or under 18 years if the child is not in employment. Germany, Portugal and Greece consider any person with never-married children living in their household, whatever the age of these children, to be a lone parent. This makes comparisons based on national definitions problematic and one of the strengths of the ECHP is that it allows us to construct the same definition across these countries.

However, agreeing an appropriate definition was not straightforward since these definitional variations suggest that there are different ideas about the nature of lone parenthood across countries, so that different types of lone-parent family may be more or less visible to policy makers. There are a number of routes into lone parenthood, for example, divorce; the breakdown of a relationship where the couple were cohabiting but not married; the death of one partner in a marriage; women who have a child or children without any permanent relationship. Different definitions will pick up these family types to varying extents. For example, if the focus is just on families with children aged under 16 or 19 (as in the UK), this means that many widows, who tend to be older and have older children, will be excluded.

Further, as shown in Chapter 3, there are significant variations in the extent to which 'older' children continue to live with their parents. In these six countries most young people between the ages of 16 and 19 years are living with their parents. This is still mainly true for young men aged 20–24, although less so for young women. But among those aged 25–29 there are clear differences across the countries. More than two-fifths of young people of this age are living with parents in Greece and Portugal compared with only around one in ten or one in seven in Norway and the UK. Germany and Austria fall somewhere between these two groups. It is more often young men than young women in their twenties who are living with parents. If this applies to lone-parent as well as couple households, then we would expect to find more lone parents living with older children in Greece and Portugal than in Norway and the UK, with Austria and Germany including both types of lone-parent household.

Table 4.1 shows the household composition of all households in the study, taking account of adult family status, whether single or a couple, and the presence of children. Three groups are shown in respect of children – those with no children at all, those with at least one child who is dependent, and those with non-dependent children only. Dependent children have been defined as those aged under 16 *or* in full-time education. This definition thus includes older children still in education, many of whom (as Chapter 3 showed) continue to live with their parents. The first of these three groups, therefore, has no current responsibility for children, although their households may have done so in the past. The second group has current caring responsibilities for at least one child, although their households may also include some older non-dependent children. The third group is living with

Table 4.1   Household type: all households (column per cent)

Household type	AT	D	GR	N	PT	UK
Couple, no children	23	27	23	29	19	27
Couple, at least one dependent child*	23	23	32	31	39	28
Couple, non-dependent children only	7	8	11	5	11	8
Single, no children	29	32	18	18	10	23
Single, at least one dependent child	3	3	2	3	4	6
Single, non-dependent children only	7	8	11	5	11	8
Other household	11	3	10	15	12	5
Total	100	100	100	100	100	100
Base (households)	3380	4688	5220	3720	4916	4548

Note: * Dependent child is defined as aged under 16 or in full-time education.

adult children, and so have had past caring responsibilities for children, but not current.

As the table shows, the broad picture across these countries is similar but with some differences between Greece and Portugal and the rest. Households consisting of couples with children make up around two-fifths of households in Greece and Portugal compared with about one-third elsewhere. Living alone as a couple is least common in Portugal (19 per cent) and most common in Norway (29 per cent). Living alone as a single person is also least common in Portugal (10 per cent) and most common in Germany (32 per cent). Multi-family households (the 'other' category in the table) are more common in Portugal, Austria and Greece than they are in the UK and Germany.

Focusing just on those with dependent children, the proportion of lone-parent households is around 2–3 per cent in Austria, Germany, Greece and Norway, slightly higher in Portugal at 4 per cent, and highest in the UK at 6 per cent of all households. However, when the proportion of all households that are headed by a lone parent is considered, regardless of the age of children, these patterns are almost reversed. The countries with the lowest proportions of this household type are Norway (5 per cent), followed by Austria, the UK and Germany (7–8 per cent), with the highest proportions found in Greece and Portugal (11 per cent). These differences reflect the different patterns of young people leaving home (as discussed briefly above and more fully in Chapter 3) and suggest the need to consider both families with dependent children and those with non-dependent children.

Table 4.2 therefore excludes childless households and shows those with children, whether dependent or non-dependent regardless of age of child. The top two lines show that, among all lone-parent households, those with at least one dependent child are clearly more numerous than those with just non-dependent children in Norway and the UK but the opposite is the case in Portugal and Greece. In both Germany and Austria, lone-parent households are divided almost half-and-half into these two family types. The table also shows the rate of lone parenthood, defined in these two different ways. First, if we focus – as many studies do – just on those with dependent children, then rates of lone parenthood are highest in the UK (18 per cent), followed by Austria (12.5 per cent), and then three countries at round 9–10 per cent (Germany, Norway and Portugal), with Greece having the lowest rate at 5.8 per cent. Secondly, if we take the wider definition and include all families regardless of age of children, then the rates of lone parenthood look much more similar across the countries. The UK still has the highest rate (20 per cent) but is closely followed by Austria (19 per cent), Portugal (16 per cent), Germany (14 per cent), Greece (13 per cent) and Norway (9 per cent).

Table 4.2   Household type: households with children (column per cent)

Household type	AT	D	GR	N	PT	UK
Lone parent households:						
– with at least one dependent child*	9	8	4	8	7	14
– with non-dependent children only	10	6	9	*	9	6
Couple households:						
– with at least one dependent child*	63	66	64	79	66	62
– with non-dependent children only	19	20	23	13	19	18
Total	100	100	100	100	100	100
Lone parents with dependent children as a % of all families with dependent children	12.5	10.8	5.8	9.0	9.5	18.0
Lone parents with children of any age as a % of all families with children of any age	19.0	14.0	13.0	9.0	16.0	20.0
Base (households)	1496	2007	2602	1450	2432	1861

Note: *Dependent children are defined as children aged under 16, or over 16 and in full-
time education.

The rates of lone parenthood (according to our two definitions) in the
ECHP dataset are not dissimilar to those found in other studies, although
there is no definitive source against which to compare these. Ditch et al.
(1996, p. 23) summarise figures from a number of datasets and conclude
that 'there are significant differentials between the various estimates; these
require further investigation'. The ECHP figures tend to be lower than the
national estimates but the order of the countries is as would be expected.
Norway, however, looks to be substantially below other national estimates.
Skevik (2001) for example, puts the Norwegian figure at 18 per cent. This
is based on numbers in receipt of the higher rate of child benefit and so
excludes cohabiting couples and those with children over 16. This is twice
as high as the figure given here, which (as noted in the Introduction to this
volume) is based not on ECHP data (Norway is not a participant) but on
the Norwegian Living Standards Survey. It is likely that this is missing lone
parents living in larger households but this would not account for all the
difference. These Norwegian figures should, therefore, be treated with some
caution.

   Although these figures may be on the low side, they do suggest that the
study countries fall broadly into three groups of two. In the UK and
Norway, lone parenthood is mainly a situation in which one parent (usually

Table 4.3   *Age and marital status: lone mothers with at least one dependent child (column per cent within category)*

	AT	D	GR	N	PT	UK
Sex						
Women	91	88	82	87	91	87
Age of lone mother						
16–29 years	[19]	*	*	20	*	35
30–44 years	62	67	[56]	62	58	56
45 plus	[19]	[19]	[39]	18	38	[9]
Marital status of lone mother						
Single, never married	[29]	[40]	*	13	*	36
Separated/Divorced	55	57	[54]	87	46	57
Widowed	*	*	[37]	–	[34]	*
Base (lone mothers)	114	136	78	104	123	220

a woman, see Table 4.3) lives with dependent children. In Portugal and Greece a significant proportion of lone parents are older women, living with children who are technically non-dependent and who may be working, studying or unemployed. These lone parents are mainly widowed. In Austria and Germany, both types of lone-parent household can be found. These variations make the policy issues facing lone parents rather different.

However, the extent to which this can be explored further is limited by the small sample sizes for these households in the ECHP. For our analysis the lone parents have been divided into two groups: those with at least one dependent child and those with non-dependent adult children only. This allows us to start to consider whether and how these demographic differences are reflected in difference in incomes and living standards and thus compare what may be very different experiences of lone parenthood in these countries. The results for both groups are shown where possible (that is when sample sizes are large enough) but in other cases we just concentrate upon the more numerous group of lone parents with at least one dependent child.

This is the case for Table 4.3, which only includes lone parents with at least one dependent child. It shows that in all six countries lone mothers form the vast majority (over 80 per cent) of these families. These lone mothers are typically aged between 30 to 44, and usually ex-married. However, there are some cross-national variations. For example, the UK has a substantial proportion (35 per cent) of lone mothers aged under 30. In Greece and Portugal around two-fifths of these women are aged over 45, probably reflecting the relatively longer range of the childbearing years in these countries compared with the north where childbearing is increasingly confined to a relatively small number of years. These two countries also include a higher proportion of widows than the other countries. Single (that is unmarried) motherhood is highest in Germany and the UK. The numbers are too small to show separately the ages and marital status of lone mothers with non-dependent children only, but in all countries these tended to be older women (aged 45 plus) and were usually widows.

To some extent these two groups of lone mothers are separate groups but they may also reflect different life-course stages of lone motherhood. Some of the older women with grown-up children would have been those who, when younger, were separated or divorced women. In countries where divorce is difficult and remarriage still rare (which would include Greece here and to some extent Portugal), women who do become lone mothers through marital breakdown may stay as lone mothers for many years. But some of these older women will be women who brought up their children in couple families and who only became lone parents on the death of their spouse, perhaps when their children were already young adults. Their long-term circumstances might be quite different.

EMPLOYMENT – PROVISIONS FOR WORKING AND NON-WORKING LONE PARENTS

The extent to which lone parents are able to support themselves through work will depend to a large extent on their ability to reconcile the demands of work and family life. For any individual lone parent the decision to work will involve consideration of a complex interplay of factors, some of which lend themselves more readily to comparative study than others. In practical terms lone parents will take into account: the availability of suitable jobs; calculation of the financial gains and losses to the family resulting from a decision to work; the availability and cost of suitable childcare; the extent to which employers make, or are required to make, special provision for workers with children. In addition less measurable psychological and sociological factors will come into play. These will include judgements about whether the child(ren) will be better served by having their parent at home or in work which, in turn, depend to some extent on societal attitudes about the relative merits of daycare and parental care and, more generally, about 'good' parenting. The policy approaches of different countries are an important factor in facilitating or limiting employment for lone parents (Millar, 1996; Lewis, 1997; Duncan and Edwards, 1999).

The type, level and conditions attached to provision for families bringing up children vary greatly among the study countries. Most countries provide some form of universal family benefit and/or insurance-based benefits conditional on the work history of the parents. Lone parents in all countries are entitled to these provisions on the same basis as other parents. Very few countries make any special provision for lone parents within the universal and/or insurance-based system. Lone parents in Austria are entitled to a higher parental leave allowance, but only if the father is named and, if the father's income exceeds certain limits, the allowance has to be repaid. However, all these countries have insurance-based widows' benefits and so some lone parents will be entitled to these, based on their husbands' contributions.

Most countries treat non-working lone parents in exactly the same way as any other worker who is unemployed. In Germany, Austria, Greece and Portugal benefit entitlement for lone parents depends on contribution records. As with family benefits, since the systems were designed to accommodate the traditional model of male breadwinner and woman childcarer, many lone mothers will either not be entitled to benefits on the basis of their own contribution record or will exhaust their entitlement if they remain out of the labour market for a lengthy period. In the UK, contribution-linked unemployment benefit has been replaced by the Job Seeker's Allowance which offers the same low basic level of benefit whether or not contribution conditions have been met. Only in Norway are lone parents entitled to a special transitional benefit, equivalent to the minimum pension, which is funded under the National Insurance system. This is currently paid for three years, with the possibility of a further two years if the lone parent is in education, and only until the child finishes her/his third year at school.

The result is that in all countries, including Norway, many non-working lone parents are dependent on the residual benefit system, or social assistance. Whilst eligibility criteria, administrative systems and the proportions of benefit recipients vary from country to country, all social assistance schemes are means-tested and provide low levels of income compared to average incomes in work and, with the exception of the UK, to work-related benefits. Again, few social assistance schemes make special provision for lone parents. In Germany lone parents on social assistance receive higher rates of benefit for their children, dependent on the age and number of children. In Austria lone parents may be entitled to a special social assistance payment if their child is under three years old. The size of this payment is, however, dependent on previous wages.

In all these countries, except the UK, receipt of social assistance for lone parents is conditional to some extent on willingness to work. In Austria, for example, the special social assistance payment available to parents whose child is under three years old is conditional on the claimant being able to prove that they cannot get work because of lack of childcare facilities. Since one-third of these payments are the responsibility of local authorities, some may claim to have childcare places available when, in fact, they do not. In Norway lone parents with children aged over three must either be seeking work, in education or engaged in some work as a condition of benefit receipt.

However the UK has recently introduced measures intended to encourage more lone parents into the labour market. In the UK, these include financial incentives to 'make work pay', including the Working Families Tax Credit, which supplements the wages of those in low-paid jobs. A national childcare strategy has been introduced for the first time and a new entitlement to unpaid parental leave (Millar, 2001 summarises these). The New Deal for Lone Parents offers information and advice to those seeking work, and New Deal interviews are to be made compulsory for lone parents from 2001.

The UK is, however, the country with the lowest labour market participation rates for lone mothers, as Tables 4.4a and 4.4b show. Table 4.4a shows lone mothers with at least one dependent children compared with married mothers in the same situation. The lone mothers' activity rates (employed plus unemployed) are by far the lowest in the UK at 29 per cent, compared with about 56 per cent for Greece, between 65 and 69 per cent for Norway, Austria and Germany, and about 77 per cent in Portugal. Norwegian lone mothers rarely define themselves as being in the category 'care at home' and the 'other' category here includes about 13 per cent who are in education or training. Comparing these activity rates with those of partnered women with dependent children shows that lone mothers are more likely than partnered mothers to be employed in all the countries except Norway and the UK. The gap in the UK is especially large, even though partnered mothers do not have very high rates of economic activity (56 per cent) compared with their counterparts in other countries, they nevertheless have much higher participation rates than UK lone mothers (29 per cent). Portugal stands out as the country with the highest participation rates for both lone and partnered mothers (77 and 72 per cent respectively).

Partnered women with non-dependent children tend to have the lowest participation rates across all the countries, as Table 4.4.a shows, with participation rates of around 38 per cent (Greece) to 46 per cent (Austria) and around 51 to 54 per cent in Norway, Portugal and Germany. However, in the UK these women have the highest participation rates of any group (71 per cent). Lone mothers with non-dependent children have higher rates of economic participation than partnered women in Austria, Germany and

Table 4.4a *Lone and married mothers with at least one dependent child:*
main activity (column per cent within category)

	AT	D	GR	N	PT	UK
Lone mothers						
Economically active	67	69	[56]	65	77	29
Care of home/family	[14]	[23]	*	11	[16]	63
Other	*	*	*	23	*	*
Partnered mother						
Economically active	63	57	47	77	72	56
Care of home/family	35	41	50	11	25	42
Other	*	*	[3]	10	[3]	*

Table 4.4b *Lone and married mothers with non-dependent children only:*
main activity (column per cent within category)

	AT	D	GR	N	PT	UK
Lone mothers						
Economically active	[67]	[65]	[49]		[34]	[63]
Care of home/family	*	*	[34]		[24]	*
Other	*	*	*		*	*
Partnered mother						
Economically active	46	54	38	51	51	71
Care of home/family	43	38	57	12	30	31
Other	[9]	*	[6]	38	15	*

Greece. In the UK participation rates are slightly lower for the lone mothers
and in Portugal they are substantially lower.

Thus in Austria, Germany and Greece, lone mothers have much the same
level of economic activity rates, regardless of whether their families include
dependent children or are all adult children. They stay in work at the same
rate, and this suggests that the households with non-dependent children are
likely to be better off, as they will probably have more than one earner and
may have several earners. Young people (as discussed in Chapter 3) tend to
have lower pay rates than older workers and suffer more unemployment.
Nevertheless many young people make a significant contribution to the
family income. In Portugal the lone mothers with adult children are much
less likely to be employed than those with dependent children. In the UK,
in contrast, the women with adult children increase their labour market

participation. Unlike younger lone mothers, women with non-dependent children are not entitled to benefit support in the UK (unless they are widowed) and this must be a factor in explaining this pattern.

Millar (1996) has argued that there are two distinct groups of countries with high levels of employment for lone mothers with dependent children. On the one hand, there are those countries that actively support employment for parents, and so high levels of employment represent responses to a more positive environment for working parents. On the other hand, there are those countries where the type and level of support offered to non-employed lone parents is very low and so there is more of a negative 'push' into work (rather than a positive pull).

In terms of parental leave schemes and childcare provision this variation can be seen across these countries. All have some statutory provision for parents to be able to take leave from employment to care for young or sick children in addition to maternity leave. However, as Table 4.5 shows, the extent of such provision varies significantly in terms of the length of parental leave allowed, the extent to which such leave is paid or unpaid, the conditions under which it is granted and, in the case of Greece, the size and sector of the organisation in which the employee works. Lone parents in all countries except Norway are treated exactly the same as each parent in a two-parent family, with the result that they are relatively disadvantaged in the total amount of leave available to the family. Looking across these countries, the UK has particularly low levels of support and Austria and Germany provide the longest periods of parental leave.

Childcare provision also varies extensively among these countries in terms of numbers of places provided, who provides the care, and the extent of state assistance with meeting childcare costs. However, very little provision exists in any country for children under three years old and in general support is patchy for older children, particularly in rural areas. Only in Norway is there, apparently, no problem. In Austria and Germany, where publicly funded childcare is, at least in part, the responsibility of the local authorities, provision is said to be variable. In Greece and Portugal levels of provision are low, although lone parents are given priority access to these.

The extent to which states provide assistance with childcare costs also varies. Norway makes a flat rate contribution plus means-tested assistance with additional costs until the child finishes the third year in school. In Greece, although there is no direct financial support, state facilities are free and municipal childcare services are means-tested. The local social assistance administration in Germany pays childcare costs for all families receiving minimum income support, and childcare costs can be set against tax liability. Local authority provision is means-tested and some not-for-profit

Table 4.5   Parental leave and childcare provision – mid 1990s

	Leave to care for sick child	Parental Leave[1]	Other provision	Publicly funded childcare (1995) 0–3 year olds 4–6 year olds (%)
AT	One week paid per annum	Up to 24 months. 18 months lone parents		3 75
D[2]	Ten days per child per annum at 70 per cent gross wage	Up to two years		2 78
GR	100+ employees Unpaid leave 1 child – 6 days 2 children – 8 days 3 or more children – ten days.	PUBLIC SECTOR Unpaid First child – up to 2 years Subsequent children – up to 1 year each PRIVATE SECTOR 3 months each parent (6 months lone parent)+	4 days per annum paid leave to visit school	3 70
N[3]	Paid leave. 15 days per annum each parent for children under 12 years (30 days lone parent)	Unpaid leave 1 year each parent each child. 2 years lone parents+	Right to unpaid reduced working hours by arrangement with employer	60+

91

Table 4.5 (*cont.*)

	Leave to care for sick child	Parental Leave[1]	Other provision	Publicly funded childcare (1995) 0–3 year olds / 4–6 year olds (%)
PT	Under ten years – 30 days per annum. Over ten years – 15 days per annum. Paid 65 per cent of average daily wage	Unpaid 6 months leave for child under 3 years old	Right to flexible hours and part-time work for children under 12	12 / 48
UK	No national provision	Unpaid leave scheme (introduced in 2000)		2 / 60

Notes:
1. Following maternity leave. In Greece – conditional on one year's employment and can be refused if more than 8 per cent of workforce take parental leave in that year. In Norway – conditional on six months employment.
2. Childcare figures for West Germany, in East Germany equivalent figures were 50 per cent and 100 per cent.
3. Childcare figures for Norway refer to percentage of children in nurseries, all under school-age children.

organisations give lone parents significant reductions in fees. Lone parents in the UK who are in receipt of Working Families Tax Credit (see above) can receive some financial assistance with childcare costs and the small number of local authority day nurseries are free. There are currently no other state subsidies available. In Portugal payments are means-tested with no special assistance for lone parents.

Thus Norway seems to have the highest levels of support for working parents (although not as high as other Nordic countries). The other countries all offer support that is limited and not very generous in level. There is therefore a heavy reliance upon informal support, particularly from other family members. This, alongside rules that do not require lone parents to seek work, helps to keep labour market participation down in the UK. Lone mothers with non-dependent children seem better able to sustain employment in the UK, although whether this is because they no longer need childcare or because they no longer have the opportunity to receive Income Support without being required to seek work is not clear. Thus, although Norway and the UK have similar demographic profiles of lone parenthood, they have very different employment patterns and policy provisions. Lone parents in Greece and Portugal do not have much support for employment but nor do they receive much by way of social assistance if they are not in work. The lone parents with non-dependent children have lower employment rates than the younger women, perhaps helped by widows' pensions. The same is true, to a lesser extent, in Germany and Austria, although these countries offer more by way of parental leave schemes and lone mothers with non-dependent children stay in the labour market to the same extent as the younger women. The employment patterns of lone parents are the result of a complex mix of factors and, as Bradshaw et al. (1996, p. 79) concluded in their major cross-national study of lone parents in twenty countries, there are no 'single or simple measures that can be used to increase the employment of lone parents in any given country'.

THE RISK OF POVERTY AND SOCIAL EXCLUSION

All previous research shows that lone parents face a high risk of poverty compared with other households (see above). In this section ECHP data are used to examine income poverty, and also multi-dimensional deprivation and social isolation.

Table 4.6 shows the proportion of non-retired individuals living in poor households (that is with equivalent household income below 60 per cent of the median). It is clear that lone mothers with dependent children in all six countries are more likely to be living in poor households than any other

Table 4.6   *Poverty rates by household type: individuals under state retirement age (cell per cent)*

Household type	AT	D	GR	N	PT	UK
Population poverty rate	15	18	20	12.5	24	20
Lone mother family:						
– with at least one dependent child	[36]	43	[39]	18	40	51
– with non-dependent children only	*	[24]	[21]	–	32	[22]
Couple family:						
– with at least one dependent child	16	19	13	8	19	18
– with non-dependent children only	[11]	14	17	5	17	[6]
Single, living alone	23	21	35	25	52	27
Couple, no children	12	12	34	9	35	15
Other	[13]	[21]	21	8	20	[23]

Note: Analysis includes all in household (adults and children).

family type. The poverty rates for lone mothers with at least one dependent child range from just over half (51 per cent) in the UK, to around one-third or two-fifths in Austria, Germany, Greece and Portugal (36–43 per cent), to under a fifth in Norway (18 per cent). Couples with dependent children tend to have higher than average poverty rates for their countries, but these are always much lower than the poverty rates of the lone mothers. The care of dependent children is a risk factor for poverty; bringing up those children on your own even more so.

Lone mothers with non-dependent children are not so much at risk of poverty as their younger counterparts and show poverty rates lower, or not much higher, than the average in Germany, Greece and the UK. In Portugal their poverty rates are higher. As discussed above, these women have relatively low employment rates and it seems that their combination of family support and widows pensions is unable to prevent poverty for a significant proportion. The high rates of poverty in the UK are also related to low employment rates.

Table 4.7 shows household items that respondents say they cannot afford – items such as adequate heating in the home, holidays, new clothes, replacing furniture, eating meat or an alternative, and having family or friends around for dinner or drinks. Looking first at the circumstances of couples with children gives an indication of the general differences across the countries. This suggests that Norway has the lowest levels of deprivation of this type, followed by Germany, Austria and the UK, with Portugal and Greece

Table 4.7   Household items cannot afford: lone mothers and couples
(cell per cent)

Families with at least one dependent child	AT	D	GR	N	PT	UK
Cannot afford to do/have:						
Lone mother						
1. Replace furniture	71	62	84	42	82	81
2. Holiday once a year	[43]	[32]	67	38	60	82
3. Warm home	*	*	55	5	62	[17]
4. New clothes	[24]	43	[55]	13	51	36
5. Meat/alternative, every other day	*	[19]	[43]	15	*	[22]
6. Friends/family for drinks/dinner	[20]	[28]	62	19	[23]	37
Couples						
1. Replace furniture	42	23	70	8	70	36
2. Holiday once a year	22	[12]	39	7	52	36
3. Warm home	3	*	32	1	59	6
4. New clothes	9	15	20	2	38	11
5. Meat/alternative, every other day	[6]	6	25	2	4	5
6. Friends/family for drinks/dinner	11	12	33	2	16	13
Families with non-dependent children						
Lone mother						
1. Replace furniture	51	[39]	84	82	*	[44]
2. Holiday once a year	[36]	[25]	57	74	*	[43]
6. Friends/family for drinks/dinner	[21]	[21]	52	31	*	24
Couples						
1. Replace furniture	46	19	80	79	*	27
2. Holiday once a year	26	[11]	57	66	*	30
6. Friends/family for drinks/dinner	14	13	49	18	*	12

Note: Analysis includes all in household (adults and children).

the highest. The items most likely to cause problems are replacing furniture and affording holidays. The item most likely to differentiate across countries is heating the home – rarely a problem in Austria, Germany and the UK but affecting a significant minority of couples with children in Greece and Portugal.

Among lone mothers with dependent children the same sort of pattern applies – Greece and Portugal have the highest deprivation scores and Norway the lowest. However, it is also clear that levels of deprivation are in general much higher for lone mothers than they are for couples with dependent children. Replacing furniture is often a problem, although less so in Norway. Having a holiday is difficult for lone mothers in the UK, Portugal and Greece. Lone mothers in these countries are likely to also find it difficult to afford new clothes. The largest gaps between the lone mothers and couples with dependent children are in Germany and Austria and the smallest in Greece and Portugal. Thus, Greece and Portugal have higher overall levels of this sort of deprivation but lower relative levels. The opposite is true for Germany and Austria.

Table 4.7 also shows how families with non-dependent children fare on three of the measures, replacing furniture, affording holidays and having family or friends for drinks or dinner (sample sizes were too small for analysis of the other items). The general picture is similar to that for families with dependent children. Greece and Portugal have the highest levels of deprivation on these measures, but this is true for both lone mothers and couples. So being a lone mother with adult children does not seem to make you substantially worse off than other families, since they too are struggling to replace furniture, to afford holidays and (to a lesser extent) to have family gatherings. For these older families it is in Germany where the largest differences between one and two parent families are to be found. For example, 39 per cent of the lone mothers with adult children said they could not afford to replace furniture compared with 19 per cent of couple families with adult children.

Comparing lone mothers with dependent children with lone mothers with adult children shows that in general those with the younger children are having greater difficulty in affording these items. However the gap between these two types of lone-parent family is not very large in Greece or in Portugal, where (as we have seen) many families have difficulties with these items. In the UK, the younger lone mothers are much more likely to be deprived on these measures than the older lone mothers, highlighting again the very poor relative circumstances of lone mothers with dependent children in the UK.

Composite scores for relative deprivation were calculated across four main areas: household amenities, household durable, housing quality and household shortcomings (except for Norway). The items included and methodology used are as described in Chapter 2. Essentially these are relative measures within each country, weighting items in order to take into account the extent of deprivation in each country. The deprivation line was set at 20 per cent, so all the population figures are close to this figure (the distributions mean that not all give exactly a 20 per cent cut off point). This means that it is not possible to use these figures to compare population rates between countries (since these are set up to be broadly the same). What the figures allow is a comparison of the relative rates for lone parents to the population as a whole within (and between) countries.

Table 4.8a   Deprivation measures: individuals under state retirement age in households with at least one dependent child (cell per cent within category)

	AT	D	GR	PT	UK
Population rates					
Deprived: household amenities	25	20	15	20	14
Deprived: household durables	19	18	18	22	21
Deprived: housing quality	20	20	17	20	20
Deprived: household necessities	19	21	21	22	20
Lone mother with at least one dependent child					
Deprived: household amenities	[23]	42	*	[22]	[15]
Deprived: household durables	39	43	[44]	[25]	64
Deprived: housing quality	[31]	[33]	*	[20]	27
Deprived: household necessities	[33]	54	[47]	[24]	56
Couple with at least one dependent child					
Deprived: household necessities	22	14	10	13	11
Deprived: household durables	18	18	12	19	18
Deprived: housing objective	23	21	15	15	23
Deprived: household necessities	16	21	12	17	18

Note: Analysis includes all in household (adults and children).
Data for Norway not available.

Table 4.8b   Deprivation measures: individuals under state retirement age in households with non-dependent children (cell per cent within category)

	AT	D	GR	PT	UK
Lone mother with non-dependent child					
Deprived: household amenities	[24]	[25]	[14]	35	[15]
Deprived: household durables	[26]	[26]	32	37	[36]
Deprived: housing quality	[20]	*	[28]	[22]	[17]
Deprived: household necessities	[27]	[36]	31	34	[31]
Couple with non-dependent child					
Deprived: household amenities	18	14	14	25	[16]
Deprived: household durables	17	13	17	24	[13]
Deprived: housing objective	[13]	19	23	23	22
Deprived: household necessities	22	18	21	20	13

Note: Analysis includes all in household (adults and children).
Data for Norway not available.

Table 4.9   Social relations: lone and married mothers with at least one dependent child (cell per cent)

Mothers with at least one dependent child	AT	D	GR	N	PT	UK
Lone mother						
Not a member of a club/organisation	78	73	90	26	94	73
Talks to neighbours < once or						
twice a month	[28]	[21]	*	55	*	[9]
Meets friends/relatives < once or						
twice a month	[30]	[18]	*	22	[24]	[13]
Partnered mother						
Not a member of a club/organisation	64	56	91	14	93	64
Talks to neighbours < once or						
twice a month	14	12	4	38	10	11
Meets friends/relatives < once or						
twice a month	33	26	10	25	30	15
Mothers with non-dependent children						
Lone: not a member of a						
club/organisation	[75]	[66]	99	–	89	[81]
Partnered: not a member of a						
club/organisation	74	53	95	15	94	53

Table 4.8a shows the results for lone mothers and couples with at least one dependent child. In general, couples with dependent children are less deprived on these measures than the population in general, with no clear patterns of cross-national difference. For lone mothers, however, there are high levels of relative deprivation in Germany, Greece and Austria. In the UK, there is little deprivation with respect to household amenities but high levels for durables and necessities. In Portugal, lone mothers with at least one dependent child do not appear to be more deprived than the population in general, but small sample sizes mean this result should be treated with caution.

Table 4.8b shows the same analysis for families with non-dependent children only. For couples the same pattern applies, those with non-dependent children have lower levels of deprivation relative to the population as a whole (and, looking back to the previous table, compared with couples with at least one dependent child). This might be expected since these are families that can have multiple earners, including older and more established wage earners. The lone mothers with non-dependent children, however, do not fare so well. Although not as relatively deprived as their counterparts with at least one dependent child, they do tend to have higher levels of deprivation than the population as a whole. This is especially true for Portugal and for the UK on the durables and necessities measures.

Finally, Table 4.9 examines measures of social relations – belonging to clubs, talking with neighbours, meeting with friends or family. There are some differences across the countries but these apply as much to married mothers with dependent children as they do to the lone mothers. For example, membership of clubs is more common in Austria, Germany and the UK than in Greece and Portugal. The pattern of club membership is much the same for women with adult children, whether lone or married. Regular contact with neighbours, family and friends is generally high, with few people reporting they lack such contact. But in Norway lone mothers are least likely to be in contact with neighbours. Greece is at the opposite end, with the number not in contact with friends or relatives being negligible.

CONCLUSIONS

These six countries show three different patterns of lone parenthood. In the UK and Norway lone parents are mainly ex-married women with dependent children, although also including some never-married women. In Portugal and Greece lone parents are more likely to be older, widowed women, with adult children. In Austria and Germany, both types of lone-parent household can be found. The situation of the older women is usually better than that of the younger women, although in Portugal these older lone parents also experience high levels of poverty and relative deprivation. Employment rates vary from a very low level in the UK to the highest levels in Portugal. The factors driving these different employment outcomes are multiple and complex, but high levels of employment are not necessarily associated with active family-friendly policies. In some cases it seems that lone parents have little choice but to enter work, since there are so few alternatives available to them. Because of small sample sizes it has not been possible to analyse these in as much detail for lone parents as for the other risk groups. But the results clearly confirm what other studies also show – high poverty risks for this family type and much relative deprivation.

There is, however, a contrast between Austria and Germany on the one hand and Greece and Portugal on the other. In Austria and Germany the risk of poverty for lone parents is closer to that for other families, but the levels of relative deprivation are higher. These lone parents are experiencing poverty and hardship in well-off societies and so their relative position is much worse. In Greece and Portugal, by contrast, although the poverty risk for lone parents is high, the same is true of other families. These lone parents are experiencing poverty in societies where poverty is not uncommon and their relative position is not so bad. However the lone parents with non-dependent children do seem to be in a very disadvantaged position in Portugal. The situation of widowed lone parents has not been the focus of much recent research attention, but the needs of these women are not necessarily being met and their poverty and deprivation is likely to be quite long in duration.

Lone parenthood in the UK is something of a special case compared with these other countries, including more younger families, without employment, and with high rates of both income poverty and deprivation. Norway provides the contrast here – similar types of families but higher levels of employment, more state support to assist working parents, and lower poverty and deprivation rates. Both countries are now concentrating policy on encouraging more lone parents into employment. Lewis (2001) suggests that more countries are moving away from a 'male-breadwinner' to an 'adult worker' model in which policy is based on the assumption that all adults – whether caring for children are not – should be in the labour market. But employment does not, as we have seen, always protect against poverty. Support for working parents – in both cash and kind – will also be required, if poverty in work is to be avoided.

5.   Sickness and disability

Christopher Heady

INTRODUCTION

Comparative analysis has paid very little attention to the circumstances of those who suffer from sickness or disability. Yet research in individual countries (for example, Amera, 1996, and Berthoud et al., 1993) shows that the onset of such conditions causes major changes in circumstances, not only for the affected individual but also for the household in which s/he lives. It is therefore appropriate to include this group in the analysis of those who run a particularly high risk of social exclusion.

This chapter starts with a discussion of policy towards the sick and disabled in the six study countries. It then presents data on the incidence of sickness and disability in each country and the characteristics of the sick and disabled. This sets the scene for an analysis of the links between sickness and disability on the one hand and poverty and deprivation on the other. Finally, a concluding section highlights the main findings.

POLICY

One of the main challenges for the comparative analyst is the extent to which definitions and classifications of sickness and disability vary between countries. In this section the definitions adopted by the countries in this study are described. The main policy provisions for this group are outlined and, finally, the policy debates in each country are considered.

Definitions

All countries have an official definition of sickness and disability that is linked to a person's ability to participate in the labour market and to eligibility for social security benefits. These definitions are usually operationalised through the application of medical criteria. The link between disability definition and labour market participation has been particularly

101

strong in Germany, where the concept of general invalidity makes an overt connection between disability and the condition of the labour market. The possibility of gainful employment for a disabled person is judged according to the availability of jobs, with the result that the extent of disability within the working population varies according to whether the labour market is 'open' or 'closed'.

Portugal is apparently the only country which strictly applies the World Health Organisation's (WHO) classification of impairment, disability and handicap. Norway uses the list of conditions in the WHO classificatory system to operationalise its legal definition of disability, which is linked to ability to earn a pensionable income. A person's general abilities, educational level, work experience, age, sex and geographical mobility are taken into account, alongside medical criteria.

UK official definitions of disability have changed with time, the most recent, in the Disability Discrimination Act of 1995, whilst not measuring disability overtly according to ability to work, contains the link by implication: 'A physical or mental impairment which has a substantial and long term adverse effect on a person's ability to carry out day-to-day activities'. Benefit entitlement is supposed to be assessed strictly on medical criteria, but accusations have been made that considerations of job availability have played a significant part in some doctors' decisions to define someone as disabled for benefit purposes.

In Greece until recently two main definitions were used by the insurance funds: objective or medical disability defined only by medical criteria and by medical committees; subjective disability based on a combination of the personal characteristics and some objective factors. This last definition was criticised for leading to favouritism and discrimination and a new law in 1990 included a definition of disability which only applies to insured persons and makes the explicit link between disability and ability to work.

> An insured person is considered as disabled when the medical committee that examines him/her testifies a serious illness or physical or mental disability which first appeared or deteriorated since the insured person affiliated with the fund and that he/her is not likely to be able to earn more than 1/3 of the normal earnings of a physiologically and mentally able worker in his/her professional category, education or training for at least one year.

Austria uses different combinations of medical criteria and assessments of degree of impairment to define disability in terms of eligibility for different benefits. Medical criteria alone are used in eligibility for attendance allowance, for example, whereas 'fitness for employment' is the main criteria for granting an invalidity pension.

Financial Provision

In all countries, with the exception of Greece, benefit provision for people with disabilities is more generous than for those without disabilities in terms of higher benefit levels, special benefits, or less strict contribution criteria. Most countries link receipt of at least some disability benefits to contributions paid through the insurance system, but the contribution criteria are less strict than for other benefits. In Germany, for example, entitlement is based on a contribution record of at least 36 months in the previous five years.

Disabled people are generally excluded from eligibility conditions which require able bodied people to participate in the labour market, although Austria and Norway require claimants to undergo a period of rehabilitation as a condition of benefit receipt. All countries allow those who are not entitled to the insurance-based disability benefits, or whose income falls below certain levels, to apply for benefits under the residual systems. In Germany, Norway, Portugal and the UK these systems provide additional payments for people with disabilities in recognition of the extra costs faced by this group, although the levels of these vary from country to country and are particularly low in Portugal. In Norway the amount of 'Basic Benefit' depends on the expenses incurred, while in the UK and Germany the same level of additional payment is made to any disabled person claiming social assistance.

Again with the exception of Greece, all countries provide some form of benefit to assist disabled people with payments to carers. In some countries these are flat rate benefits (Portugal's Third Persons Benefit), or paid at only two or three different levels, as in the UK (Disability Living Allowance). In Norway, Germany and Austria the level of benefit is assessed according to need. The UK also provides a special carer's benefit to recompense carers for the fact that they are unable to work because of their caring responsibilities. Both the UK's and Germany's system of payment for carers cover the national insurance costs of the carer, thereby protecting their future pension rights.

Benefit levels vary according to the extent of disability only in Norway and, to a much lesser extent, the UK. In Norway the Graded Disability Pension is calculated according to the capacity for work and is progressively reduced for those whose incapacity is between 100 per cent and 50 per cent. The pension is also available to disabled women at home to cover the expenses of employing someone to do housework, although a full disability pension is rarely paid. In the UK the Disability Living Allowance is paid at a number of different rates according to the purpose of the benefit (need for assistance with mobility or with personal care) and the degree of disability.

Some benefit systems discourage disabled people from taking employment because of conditions attached to benefit receipt. In Norway relatively low earnings can lead to large reductions in pensions, and disabled people are reluctant to try working because failure and return to benefit might be difficult in the light of new, tighter, eligibility criteria. People in receipt of a disability benefit in the UK are allowed to take up limited employment only if it can be shown to be of therapeutic value: few do. The systems in Austria, Germany and Portugal allow for little, if any, carry over of disability benefits into work.

Yet it is clear that many disabled people are capable and willing to undertake some work. Norway and the UK have recognised this by making some provision to assist disabled people into work. Norway's rehabilitation benefit is a transitional benefit, similar to that provided for lone parents, which aims to assist disabled people back into work. In addition, disabled people are allowed to return to work for a trial period of up to 12 months during which time their right to a pension is frozen, rather than removed. The Disability Working Allowance in the UK is an in-work benefit which supplements income from earnings and aims to ensure that people are better off in work than out of work. The new government in the UK has also made disabled people one of the target groups under the 'New Deal', alongside young long-term unemployed people and lone parents. The programme aims to provide a range of additional assistance to those seeking work.

Anti-Discrimination Laws

Very few countries make provision to defend the rights of disabled people in relation to work, and such provisions tend to lack teeth or are not enforced. Greece, Austria and Germany have no specific anti-discrimination legislation. Portugal has fairly extensive legislation, supposedly guaranteeing the constitutional rights of disabled people, but very little practical implementation of these laws has taken place. In Norway employees who become disabled have the right to be reassigned to a more appropriate job, but there is no anti-discrimination legislation to protect those not in work. Recent legislation in the UK promises new rights to, and protections for, disabled people in relation to the labour market. However, many of the provisions are not to be implemented for some time, and disability lobby groups believe that the legislation is inadequate and lacks teeth.

Some countries have legislative quotas for the percentage of disabled workers which companies are expected to employ. The quota regimes vary according to the size of companies to which they apply, the proportions of able bodied to disabled workers, and the penalties that can be applied to companies who fail to meet their quota. In Germany, for example, 6 per cent of a company's work force must be made up of disabled people, otherwise a fine is payable for each unoccupied place. However, the level of the fine is so low that many companies choose to pay the fine rather than take on disabled workers.

All countries except Greece have policies that offer companies financial inducements to employ disabled people, in the form of wage subsidies and/or assistance with adaptations to the work place. Again, the extent to which these policies are implemented and actively pursued varies. Portugal, for example, has a battery of incentives to encourage employers to take on disabled people, but it is reported that these have had little effect to date.

Rehabilitation and Special Employment Provision

Government programmes to assist disabled people back into work or to provide protected employment outside of the labour market exist in all countries. However, the emphasis on rehabilitation and re-integration varies. In some countries, such as Norway and Austria, receipt of disability benefit is conditional on the claimant undergoing a period of rehabilitation, although in Norway the rules are lenient in practice – especially for older applicants. A range of provision exists in Portugal for rehabilitation and training of disabled people, but only a relatively small number of places are provided and many of the schemes are in their infancy. Rehabilitation services in Greece are rudimentary in many areas, with only basic attempts at reintegration and re-education by the Ministry of Labour. In the UK disabled people are not currently required to participate in rehabilitation or re-training and provision is limited.

A Family or Government Responsibility?

All countries rely to a large extent on families to care for their disabled members and this responsibility falls largely on women. In Greece, for example, most disabled men are cared for by their partners, whereas most disabled women are dependent on their children for support and care. Women who care for disabled family members, and are unable to work as a result, fail to build up their own benefit entitlement. The role of carers has been recognised recently, often following intervention from the European Union, by the provision of carers' benefits. In some countries carers' insurance contributions are protected (for example Germany and the UK) but, either as carers or as disabled people themselves, women are likely to face greater difficulties than men when long-term ill health or disability strikes.

Policy Debate

In those countries with well-developed systems of financial provision for disabled people, the relative generosity of disability benefits, combined with high levels of long-term unemployment among older workers, have led governments, employers and workers themselves to use the disability route as a substitute for early retirement. Governments benefit in the short term through the apparent reduction in the unemployment figures. Employers are able to reduce their workforce at lower costs and workers are enabled effectively to leave the labour market, often with a higher level of income that is guaranteed for a longer period than unemployment benefit.

However, the resulting growth in the cost of disability benefits has caused governments to rethink provision for disabled people. Claims that the systems are being 'abused' have led to tighter eligibility criteria or a complete change in the system of provision, despite governments having either actively encouraged or, at the very least, turned a 'blind eye' to the very 'abuse' which they now seek to eliminate.

Hard evidence of widespread abuse is difficult to come by. Tighter administrative criteria and new medical criteria in the UK are together estimated to have caused 220 000 people to leave sickness and disability benefits. Their destinations are unclear. There are unconfirmed suspicions in Germany that women with no entitlement to work-related pensions have used the system of disability pensions as a substitute. The German Government has limited sickness benefits to 70 per cent of previous income, leaving some families with incomes below the social assistance limits. They also intend to break the link between the condition of the labour market and disability by transferring all responsibility for disability and sickness to social assistance. In Austria eligibility for the early old age pension on grounds of partial disability has been restricted. Norway has placed a greater emphasis on medical criteria in recent years, restricting the conditions that grant eligibility to disability pensions.

The emphasis in Portugal and Greece, where provision is underdeveloped and benefit levels are very low, is somewhat different. Greece has been concerned to promote fairness of treatment between people claiming from the different insurance funds. Portugal is attempting to develop nationwide systems of care, education and rehabilitation for disabled people and a fundamental review of provision for disabled people is under way.

THE INCIDENCE OF SICKNESS AND DISABILITY

The purpose of this section is to describe the incidence of sickness and disability, and some basic socio-demographic characteristics of this group, in the six study countries. This lays the basis for the analysis in the next section of the vulnerability of this group to poverty, deprivation and the risk of social exclusion. For the sake of comparability, we do not use the national definitions of sickness and disability are not used. Instead, somebody is defined as sick or disabled if, in answering the ECHP questions, they either say that their health in general is 'very bad' or that they are hampered 'severely' in daily activities.

The analysis in this section and the next is confined to people who are adults (age 16 years or over) and below state retirement age. The reason for the first restriction is that the ECHP does not ask the necessary questions of people under 16. The reason for the second is that it avoids confounding the difficulties of sickness and disability with those of old age. The circumstances of retired people are the subject of the next chapter.

Table 5.1 reports the incidence of sickness and disability by age and sex for the study countries. This shows a very marked increase in incidence with age. It also shows that, with the exception of the UK and Norway, men are at least as likely to be sick or disabled as women in the same age group. The only substantial difference between countries is that Portugal has the highest incidence, and this is particularly strong in proportionate terms in the younger age groups.

Table 5.1 *Incidence of sickness or disability by age and sex: adults below state retirement age (cell per cent, for example proportion of males aged 16–29 years who are sick or disabled)*

	AT		D		GR		N		PT		UK	
	M	F	M	F	M	F	M	F	M	F	M	F
16–29 years	1	1	1	1	1	0	1	4	3	3	1	2
30–44 years	3	3	2	2	3	2	6	8	5	5	3	4
45 years to SRA	9	7	12	8	8	6	16	18	12	12	9	8

Note: Less than 5 per cent missing data.

Table 5.2 reports the distribution of sick and disabled people by household type, and compares that with the distribution of other adults in the same age range. For all countries except Portugal, the largest proportion of sick and disabled people live with a partner and no children, presumably because they have mainly reached an age where their children have left home. However, in the UK a similar proportion lives with a partner and at least one dependent child, and in Greece a similar proportion lives with all

Table 5.2   Household type: adults with a sickness or disability
(column per cent within category)

	AT	D	GR	PT	UK
Adults with a sickness or disability					
Single	[9]	[19]	*	[4]	21
With partner, no children	28	42	26	15	26
Couple with at least one dependent child	[12]	18	22	31	26
Lone parent with at least one dependent child	*	*	*	*	*
Couple with all non-dependent children	[15]	[14]	26	24	[13]
Lone parent with all non-dependent children	*	*	*	*	*
Other	[24]	[3]	15	17	*
Adults without a sickness or disability					
Single	9	12	4	2	7
With partner, no children	18	23	10	10	22
Couple with at least one dependent child	36	41	45	48	41
Lone parent with at least one dependent child	3	3	2	4	5
Couple with all non-dependent children	13	14	20	15	14
Lone parent with all non-dependent children	[3]	2	4	5	3
Other	19	5	14	17	6

Notes:
Less than 5 per cent missing data.
Data for Norway not available.

non-dependent children. In Portugal, the largest proportion live with a partner and at least one dependent child, reflecting the higher proportion of younger people amongst Portugal's sick and disabled.

In the UK, sick and disabled people are substantially more likely to be single than are other adults in the same age range. There is a smaller difference in Germany, a much smaller difference in Portugal, and no difference in Austria. This has important implications in terms of both the availability of a carer and the presence of an additional wage earner in the household. Thus, on two counts, the sick and disabled appear to be particularly vulnerable. Further analysis of household type by sex (not in the table) shows that in Germany it is mainly women who run the higher risk of being single, while in the UK it is mainly men. Lone parents with dependent children are in a similarly vulnerable position, but there are insufficient numbers of those who are sick and disabled to draw any inferences here.

A slightly different way of looking at their living arrangements is to analyse marital status, as shown in Table 5.3. In all countries except the UK, the sick and disabled are more likely to be married than other adults. In all countries, they are less likely to be single, never married. This pattern can be expected from Table 5.1, which showed that sick and disabled people are generally older than other adults. It is interesting that in Germany and Portugal, those sick and disabled are more likely to be married, although they are also more likely to live alone.

Table 5.3   Marital status: adults with a sickness or disability
(column per cent within category)

	AT	D	GR	N	PT	UK
Adults with a sickness or disability						
Married	61	68	74	56	67	61
Cohabiting	*	[6]	*	12	*	*
Separated	*	*	*	26	*	*
Divorced	*	[11]	*	–	*	[15]
Widowed	*	*	*	–	[4]	*
Single, never married	19	[12]	19	7	22	[11]
Adults without a sickness or disability						
Married	57	64	68	50	64	64
Cohabiting	8	6	1	17	2	8
Separated	[1]	1	[1]	12	1	2
Divorced	5	4	2	–	2	6
Widowed	2	1	2	–	2	1
Single, never married	28	23	27	21	29	20

Notes:
Less than 5 per cent missing data.
The figure for single, never married for Norway includes those who are divorced or widowed.

Table 5.4 presents data on the educational attainment of sick and disabled people and for other adults. In all countries those who are sick and disabled are substantially more likely to have less than second stage secondary education than other adults. This is likely to be the result of three factors: that less educated people work in more dangerous occupations, that sick and disabled people are older and older people are typically less

Table 5.4   Education: adults with a sickness or disability
(column per cent within category)

Highest education level:	AT	D	GR	PT	UK
Adults with a sickness or disability					
Third	*	[15]	*	*	[13]
Second stage secondary	**	47	**	*	28
Less than second stage secondary	45	38	79	94	59
Adults without a sickness or disability					
Third	7	21	21	6	23
Second stage secondary	67	52	32	15	36
Less than second stage secondary	26	27	48	79	40

Notes:
Less than 5 per cent missing data.
Data for Norway not available.
Here, and in subsequent tables, '**' indicates that the number is not presented to ensure that the percentage for a small sample cell cannot be deduced from the column total.

well educated, and that some disabled people may have found it harder to attend school or university.

Table 5.5 presents data on main activity status. This shows that in all countries, sick and disabled people are less likely to be in employment and are more likely to be retired (even though they are below state retirement age) than other adults. Lower participation in work was to be expected, but it is interesting to note that they are so much more likely to be retired. These are the sorts of numbers that have stimulated the policy debate on whether disability pensions have been granted too freely.

THE RISK OF POVERTY AND SOCIAL EXCLUSION

The data presented in the previous section suggest that sick and disabled people are vulnerable to poverty and social exclusion because they are relatively poorly educated, less likely to be in work and more likely to live alone than other adults. The purpose of this section is to analyse the extent to which this is true, to identify the most immediate causes of deprivation and consider the role of social and private transfers in mitigating these problems.

Table 5.6 shows that, as expected, sick and disabled people have a higher poverty rate than other adults in all the study countries. In addition, with the exception of Norway, they have a higher poverty rate than the population as

Table 5.5   Main activity: adults with a sickness or disability
(column per cent within category)

	AT	D	GR	N	PT	UK
Adults with a sickness or disability						
In employment	39	26	21	22	31	[20]
Education/training	*	*	*	4	*	*
Unemployed	[10]	[12]	*	5	**	*
Care of home/family	[9]	[10]	18	8	14	35
Retired	34	46	30	56	25	36
Other	*	*	28	3	23	*
Adults without a sickness or disability						
In employment	71	70	58	68	69	72
Education/training	7	6	8	15	10	4
Unemployed	3	6	9	6	6	6
Care of home/family	12	13	19	4	9	15
Retired	6	5	5	5	5	3
Other	1	1	2	3	1	*

Note: Less than 5 per cent missing data.

Table 5.6   Income poverty: adults with a sickness or disability
(cell per cent within category, unless specified)

	AT	D	GR	N	PT	UK
Adults with a sickness or disability						
Poverty rate	[18]	20	32	11	32	22
Foster et al. (a = 1)	5.5	6.9	10.1	2.7	11.0	6.4
Foster et al. (a = 2)	2.5	3.9	4.9	1.3	5.7	2.8
Adults without a sickness or disability						
Poverty rate	16	15	16	10	18	14
Foster et al. (a = 1)	5.1	5.0	5.0	3.3	6.4	3.6
Foster et al. (a = 2)	2.5	2.5	2.4	1.7	3.5	1.5
All individuals (adults and children)						
Poverty rate	17	18	21	13	24	21
Foster et al. (a = 1)	5.4	5.7	7.1	3.3	7.9	5.3
Foster et al. (a = 2)	2.6	2.9	3.5	1.5	4.1	2.2

Note: Less than 5 per cent missing data.

a whole (including children and people above state retirement age). Additional poverty for those sick and disabled is particularly high in Greece and Portugal. In contrast, they are particularly well protected in Norway.

Table 5.7 analyses the characteristics of sick and disabled people that are associated with poverty. It reports the odds ratios for a range of socio-economic characteristics, derived from logistic regressions on whether individuals fall below the poverty line. For each country, these odds ratios are shown both for those who are sick and disabled and for other adults.

The effect of being female is to reduce the odds of the non-sick being in poverty in all countries except Portugal (where there is no effect), although this is never statistically significant. This contrasts with a simple tabulation of poverty rates by gender (not shown), where women appear to be more likely to be poor in all countries. The reason for this difference is that the logistic regression shows the *marginal* effect of the variable, controlling for the other variables in the table. Women must be more likely than men to fall into other socio-economic categories that the logistic regression shows to increase the chance of being in poverty.

The effect of gender on poverty is stronger among sick and disabled people, with only the UK showing sick and disabled women to run a higher risk of poverty. Nonetheless, there are only two countries in which sick and disabled women have a statistically significant reduction in the odds of being poor: Germany and Greece.

The effect of age on the chances of sick and disabled people being poor are mixed in Table 5.7, and it is never statistically significant. The age range in which a sick and disabled person appears least likely to be poor is over 45 in Austria, Germany and the UK, and under 30 in Greece and Portugal. This is quite a different pattern from the effects of age on poverty for other adults.

The effect of marital status on poverty among sick and disabled people is also complex. The single, never married are less likely to be poor in all countries except the UK (and a similar but less strong pattern is shown for other adults). However, for many of this group, this effect is substantially offset by the increased odds of poverty for those who live alone (with the UK again being the sole exception). This shows that it is living alone that increases the vulnerability of sick and disabled people to poverty, not the fact of being unmarried. Where marital status does play a role is in the lone parent category: this increases the risk of poverty in all countries for both those sick and disabled and other adults. However, the effect is particularly large, and statistically significant, for sick and disabled people in Germany. It is also worth noting that its effect is smaller for those who are sick and disabled than for other adults in Austria, Greece and the UK.

Table 5.7 shows the importance of education for avoiding poverty. Third

Table 5.7 Poverty by socio-economic characteristics: adults with a sickness or disability (Logit model [Exp(B)])

	AT		D		GR		PT		UK	
	Sic	NS	Sic	NS	Sic	NS	Sic	NS	Sic	NS
Sex										
Male	–	–	–	–	–	–	–	–	–	–
Female	0.74	0.99	**0.39**	0.98	**0.36**	0.89	0.85	1.00	1.58	0.84
Age										
16–29 years	–	–	–	–	–	–	–	–	–	–
30–44 years	0.52	1.23	0.29	**0.77**	2.41	**0.77**	1.19	1.21	1.48	0.98
45 years to SRA	0.22	1.00	0.28	0.80	3.23	**0.81**	1.23	1.03	0.37	**0.45**
Marital status										
Married, cohabiting	–	–	–	–	–	–	–	–	–	–
Separated, divorced	0.65	0.85	**0.07**	**0.64**	0.21	1.46	0.56	1.15	5.85	0.70
Widowed	0.11	**0.26**	0.00	**0.36**	0.37	1.00	**2.99**	**1.50**	0.01	0.50
Single never married	0.26	**0.71**	0.32	**0.60**	0.89	0.94	0.86	**1.35**	1.15	**0.37**
Household type										
With partner, no children	–	–	–	–	–	–	–	–	–	–
Alone	2.53	**2.50**	**37.5**	3.48	**7.14**	1.35	**5.78**	0.97	0.25	**4.14**
Couple with children	0.84	**1.50**	**2.27**	1.80	0.53	0.84	**0.39**	**0.56**	**6.14**	**1.33**
LP with children	1.09	**1.94**	**109**	5.20	1.06	**1.75**	1.02	1.01	1.21	**6.54**
Other	1.30	0.85	0.00	2.61	0.51	**1.29**	0.25	**0.50**	3.55	**2.02**

Table 5.7 (cont.)

	AT		D		GR		PT		UK	
	Sic	NS	Sic	NS	Sic	NS	Sic	NS	Sic	NS
Education										
Second stage secondary	–	–	–	–	–	–	–	–	–	–
Third	0.01	0.95	0.52	**0.73**	0.00	**0.53**	0.00	**0.24**	0.52	**0.40**
Less than second stage secondary	**2.27**	**1.31**	1.03	1.14	**4.17**	**2.89**	1.98	**2.47**	0.79	**1.64**
Main activity										
Employment	–	–	–	–	–	–	–	–	–	–
Education or training	0.01	**2.31**	0.84	**2.02**	0.00	**1.85**	**11.9**	1.10	**0.01**	**3.19**
Unemployed	0.84	**1.87**	**7.51**	**2.16**	**6.95**	2.79	1.34	**1.43**	**3.36**	**5.06**
Care of home/family	2.60	**1.78**	**5.09**	**1.56**	**6.24**	1.61	1.44	**2.37**	15.6	**3.80**
Retired	1.14	0.68	1.60	1.29	2.09	1.05	0.96	1.19	22.2	**4.17**
Other	0.74	**2.02**	**5.38**	**2.90**	**5.53**	**1.75**	1.12	**2.43**	**0.01**	2.32

Notes:
Less than 5 per cent missing data.
Data for Norway not available.
Key:
Sic – Adults (below state retirement age) with a sickness or disability.
NS – Adults (below state retirement age) without a sickness or disability.
Numbers in bold are statistically significant at the 5% level.

level education reduces the chances of being poor in all countries, for both sick and disabled people and other adults. Similarly, less than second stage secondary education increases the chances of poverty everywhere except the UK, where the effect on those sick and disabled is in the unexpected direction but statistically insignificant.

Table 5.7 also demonstrates the importance of employment for avoiding poverty. Those who care for the home or family have increased chances of poverty in all countries. The same is true for the retired except in Portugal, and the unemployed except in Austria. The only identified activity other than employment that reduces poverty in most of the countries is education or training. However, the causation could be the other way, with only the non-poor being able to afford education.

Table 5.8 presents similar results to Table 5.7, but the main activity status has been removed as an explanatory variable. This is because main activity status could be thought of as a choice variable that is determined by the other variables in the equation. If this were true, its inclusion in Table 5.7 would lead to biased estimates of the overall effect of those other variables on the odds of being in poverty. One of the variables that is most likely to affect activity status is education, and a comparison of table 5.8 with table 5.7 shows an increased effect of less than second stage secondary education in Germany, Greece and the UK. It also shows an increased effect of third level education in Austria. However, the effects are generally small, even when they are in the expected direction. The same can be seen to be true for the other groups of variables. Thus, the main conclusions from the discussion of Table 5.7 continue to hold.

The analysis of this chapter indicates strongly that it is their lower rate of employment that is largely responsible for the higher rate of poverty amongst sick and disabled people. In addition, this low rate of employment implies that sick and disabled people are more reliant on non-employment sources of income: private transfers, pensions and other social transfers. The extent of this reliance is shown in Table 5.9, which shows how effective such transfers are in preventing poverty for sick and disabled people and for other adults. This is achieved by showing what happens to poverty rates if particular income sources are withdrawn. For example, for those who are sick and disabled in Austria, the removal of pensions as an income source would increase the poverty rate from 18 per cent to 40 per cent. It should be noted that, as poverty is calculated for households rather than individuals, the transfers that are removed might include transfers to members of the household who are not sick or disabled.

Table 5.9 shows that the removal of pensions would produce a substantial increase in poverty for sick and disabled people in all countries, although the increase is relatively modest for the UK. These increases in poverty are

Table 5.8 Poverty by socio-economic characteristics (not main activity): adults with a sickness or disability (Logit model [Exp(B)])

	AT		D		GR		PT		UK	
	Sic	NS	Sic	NS	Sic	NS	Sic	NS	Sic	NS
Sex										
Male	–		–		–		–		–	
Female	0.96	1.16	0.56	1.09	0.62	1.14	1.00	1.23	1.72	1.07
Age										
16–29 years	–		–		–		–		–	
30–44 years	0.55	1.08	0.49	0.73	2.04	0.67	0.89	1.22	1.19	0.89
45 years to SRA	0.24	0.86	0.40	0.80	2.85	0.71	0.96	1.14	0.81	0.47
Marital status										
Married, cohabiting	–		–		–		–		–	
Separated, divorced	0.49	0.84	0.18	0.68	0.49	1.38	0.55	1.13	1.04	0.77
Widowed	0.12	0.28	0.00	0.39	0.71	1.02	2.69	1.44	0.34	0.70
Single never married	0.21	0.76	0.46	0.67	1.50	1.09	0.87	1.33	0.25	0.45
Household type										
With partner, no children	–		–		–		–		–	
Alone	2.97	2.48	17.7	3.12	2.48	1.28	5.35	0.92	4.25	4.15
Couple with children	0.95	1.60	1.85	1.80	0.53	0.86	0.39	0.53	5.84	1.48
LP with children	1.37	1.88	34.9	4.98	0.87	1.75	1.15	0.95	9.03	7.70
Other	1.49	0.85	0.00	2.60	0.55	1.26	0.23	0.48	6.29	2.06

Education

Second stage secondary	–	–	–	–	–	–	–	–	–	–
Third	0.00	0.92	0.63	**0.67**	0.00	**0.48**	0.00	**0.22**	0.62	**0.38**
Less than second stage secondary	**2.24**	**0.42**	1.25	1.16	**5.00**	**2.81**	1.06	**2.55**	1.15	**1.89**

Notes:
Less than 5 per cent missing data.
Data for Norway not available.
Key:
Sic – Adults (below state retirement age) with a sickness or disability.
NS – Adults (below state retirement age) without a sickness or disability.
Numbers in bold are statistically significant at the 5% level.

Table 5.9 *Effectiveness of household social and private transfers in preventing poverty: adults with a sickness or disability (cell per cent (poverty rates) within category)*

Annual equivalised income calculated as:	AT	D	GR	PT	UK
Adults with a sickness or disability					
Total income	18	20	32	32	22
Total income – pensions	40	40	53	42	27
Total income – other social transfers	36	–	39	41	65
Total income – private transfers	[20]	–	33	33	22
Total income – pensions and other social transfers	59	–	58	50	70
Total income – other social and private transfers	37	–	40	42	65
Total income – pensions, other social and private transfers	60	–	60	51	70
Adults without a sickness or disability					
Total income	16	15	16	18	14
Total income – pensions	25	21	24	24	17
Total income – other social transfers	24	–	17	22	24
Total income – private transfers	17	–	17	18	15
Total income – pensions and other social transfers	33	–	25	28	27
Total income – other social and private transfers	25	–	18	23	24
Total income – pensions, other social and private transfers	34	–	26	28	27

Note: Less than 5 per cent missing data.
Data for Norway not available.

much larger than those for other adults, illustrating the greater dependence on pensions among sick and disabled people. The removal of other social transfers has a similar effect, but the pattern between countries is different. For example, the effect of social transfers is much smaller than pensions in Greece, but the reverse in true for the UK. This probably reflects a greater use of pensions to assist sick and disabled people in Greece, and a greater use of other social transfers in the UK, with Austria and Portugal being somewhere in between. Private transfers have relatively little effect on the incidence of poverty. However, it might be the case that many private transfers are in kind (caring, for example) rather than cash, and so are not shown in the figures. Nonetheless, it is clear that state provision for those who are sick and disabled is of great importance in all of the study countries.

The other figures in Table 5.9 show the effect of withdrawing combinations of transfers. These confirm the minor role of private transfers, and show that pensions and other social transfers combine to raise more people out of poverty than either one on their own.

The reason for being interested in income poverty, as discussed so far in this section, is the belief that such poverty can lead to material deprivation and increase the risk of social exclusion. The remainder of this section considers the extent to which this true.

Table 5.10 reports the incidence of material deprivation for sick and disabled people and for other adults, distinguishing between the poor (P) and the non-poor (NP). With the exception of housing quality for those who are sick and disabled, the poor always have a higher level of material deprivation than the non-poor. However, with few exceptions, poor sick and disabled people suffer higher levels of material deprivation than other poor adults. Also, non-poor sick and disabled people suffer higher levels of material deprivation than other non-poor adults. Thus, while poverty does affect material deprivation, the relationship is not as simple as one might think. In particular, those who are sick and disabled appear to suffer greater material deprivation than would be expected from their poverty incidence. This could be due to lower incomes for people who are sick and disabled within both the poor and the non-poor, but it might also be a reflection of greater material needs associated with sickness and disability (for example, in order to allow mobility). This would divert funds from improving the material conditions measured in the table, and so increase material deprivation. In other words, sick and disabled people may be disadvantaged not only from a lack of income but also from increased needs.

The seriousness of the material deprivation of many sick and disabled people raises the question of whether this hinders their participation in society and thus poses the risk of social exclusion. One measure of this is the extent to which it curtails their social relations. Table 5.11 reports the proportions of sick and disabled people and of other adults who have low levels of social relations, as measured by three characteristics, distinguishing between the poor and the non-poor. This shows that, with a few exceptions, poor people are less likely to be a member of a club or organisation and are more likely to meet friends or relatives less than once or twice a month. The effects of poverty on talking to neighbours less than once or twice a month are less consistent, probably because this is an activity that is less likely to involve financial costs. Table 5.11 also shows that, generally, sick and disabled people have less active social relations than other adults, even controlling for whether or not they are poor. This could partly be the result of their disability making social activities more difficult, but the

Table 5.10   Material deprivation and income poverty: adults with a sickness or disability (cell per cent within category)

	AT		D		GR		PT		UK	
	P	NP	P	NP	P	NP	P	NP	P	NP
Adults with a sickness or disability										
'Deprived' of household amenities	[38]	[14]	[41]	22	[30]	[13]	45	21	*	[18]
'Deprived' of household durables	[53]	[21]	[42]	24	[35]	[21]	55	20	[52]	30
'Deprived' of housing quality	*	[23]	*	24	[28]	29	33	28	[54]	30
'Deprived' of household luxuries	[48]	26	[79]	26	60	33	45	26	[67]	38
Adults without a sickness or disability										
'Deprived' of household amenities	22	13	30	17	23	10	35	12	22	11
'Deprived' of household durables	27	19	33	23	38	16	43	12	42	12
'Deprived' of housing quality	24	20	24	19	23	17	24	18	29	18
'Deprived' of household luxuries	24	16	32	15	35	13	35	14	42	11

Note:
Less than 5 per cent missing data.
Data for Norway not available.

Table 5.11 Social relations by income poverty: adults with a sickness or disability (cell per cent within category)

	AT		D		GR		PT		UK	
	P	NP	P	NP	P	NP	P	NP	P	NP
Adults with a sickness or disability										
Not a member of a club or an organisation	[70]	60	[68]	55	95	92	93	89	[69]	63
Talks to neighbours less than once or twice a month	*	[24]	*	20	*	[14]	[10]	[14]	*	[10]
Meets friends/relatives less than once or twice a month	*	35	[41]	28	[29]	[17]	27	33	*	[20]
Adults without a sickness or disability										
Not a member of a club or an organisation	61	54	55	46	94	89	89	81	67	51
Talks to neighbours less than once or twice a month	26	22	20	19	3	6	9	13	12	17
Meets friends/relatives less than once or twice a month	29	27	27	25	10	9	30	26	14	15

Notes:
Less than 5 per cent missing data.
Data for Norway not available.

findings from Table 5.10 suggest that it might also be because those who are sick and disabled are more financially deprived than the poverty measures suggest, because their needs are greater.

CONCLUSIONS

This chapter has reviewed policies towards sick and disabled people by the six study countries, has presented basic descriptive statistics about this vulnerable group and has analysed the poverty and deprivation that they face.

The first main conclusion from this analysis is that policies in all countries have not prevented sick and disabled people from experiencing greater deprivation than other adults, despite the much greater reliance that sick and disabled people are able to have on social transfers. There are variations between countries in the protection offered to sick and disabled people, with Norway showing both the lowest level of poverty amongst the sick and disabled and the smallest difference in poverty between them and the rest of the population. However, in all the countries, sick and disabled people are more likely to be poor than other adults, are more likely to suffer material deprivation and are more likely to have limited social relations.

The main causes of the greater poverty of sick and disabled people are lower rates of employment, lower educational qualifications and (in some countries) a greater chance of living alone. It appears that it is lack of employment that is the most important cause. However, the material and social deprivation that this group suffers is not simply a result of income poverty. The most likely explanation of this is that sick and disabled people have greater financial needs if they are to participate fully in society, and this is not reflected in measures of income poverty. This implies that the challenge to social policy in this area is not simply to reduce the incidence of poverty among sick and disabled people to that among the general adult population. There is a need to provide additional financial resources to address their extra needs.

6. Transition into retirement

Sue Middleton

The current and projected cost of retirement to public expenditure budgets is causing concern in all the countries in this study, provoking fundamental reviews of the extent and nature of provision. The increased cost to national exchequers of retirement is the result of a so-called 'demographic time bomb' in Western Europe caused by:

1. increased life expectancy;
2. the prospective growth in the population of retired people because of increased birth rates in the post-war years; and
3. the subsequent decline in birth rates leading to a reduction in the size of the working population available to fund pension and other provision for retired people (see Chapter 3).

To this list should be added the increasing desire of people to work for shorter periods of time and the encouragement, or at least permissiveness, by governments in the 1980s and early 1990s of early retirement as a solution to problems of unemployment.

In this chapter characteristics of the 'retired' population in the study countries are described followed by a comparison of policy responses designed to meet the needs of elderly people in each country. The extent and causes of poverty among the retired are examined and, finally, the appropriateness of policy responses to the 'greying' of the European population.

The 'retired' population in this analysis, for all countries except Norway, includes adults over the age of 45 years who described themselves as retired, and people who did not claim to be retired but who were over the state retirement age and not working more than 16 hours per week. There are two main reasons for this somewhat complex definition of retirement. First, the lower age of 45 years was chosen because we wished to include in the analysis people who had retired 'early' in each country. Second, many women over the state retirement age failed to describe themselves as 'retired', since they were not in paid employment prior to reaching the state retirement age. To exclude these groups would significantly distort the make up of the retired population. The definition of 'retirement' for Norway includes people over the age of 45 years and in receipt of an old age pension (public or private). This more restrictive definition means that the Norwegian retired group in our analysis is not strictly comparable to those in other countries.

CHARACTERISTICS OF RETIRED PEOPLE

Retired people as a proportion of the population are increasing in Europe. Chapter 3 has already suggested that the proportions of young people in the study countries are getting smaller with each successive age cohort. In addition, people are living longer, having fewer children and wanting to work for shorter periods of time. It is estimated that Norway, for example, will have only two workers to every retired pensioner by the year 2030, compared with three workers in 1970. The UK will have 2.7 workers to every pensioner in 2030, compared with 3.7 workers in 1970.

In four of the six study countries retired adults form a larger percentage of the population than young people aged 16–29 years, with the gap being particularly large in Germany and Greece who also have the largest proportions of retired people in their populations (Table 6.1). The problem is less severe in the UK and, particularly, in Austria. Portugal, in contrast to the other five countries, still has a smaller proportion of retired than of young people.

The retired population as a proportion of the total is growing, not only because of declining populations in the youngest age groups, but also because retired people are living longer. Between approximately one-quarter and one-half of retired people in each country for which data are available are aged 75 years or older (Table 6.2). There are also differences in the proportions of men and women in each successive age group. Whereas there are more retired men than retired women in the 45–64 year age groups in four of the six countries, and differences in the other two are very small, there are more women than men in the oldest age group in all countries except Greece.

This longer life expectancy of women is reflected in the marital status of retired men and women (Table 6.3). Far more retired men than women are living with a partner in each country. Retired women, in contrast, are far more likely than men to be separated, divorced or single, and widowed. This pattern of large proportions of very elderly widowed women living alone has major implications for policies towards retired people (see further below).

Chapter 3 has described policies to increase levels of educational achieve-

Table 6.1   Retired and young people in the population (cell per cent)

	AT	D	GR	N	PT	UK
Retired adults	27	29	30	16	23	26
Young people 16–29 years	26	19	21	27	25	21

Table 6.2   Age and sex of retired adults (column per cent)

	AT		D		GR		N		PT		UK	
	M	F	M	F	M	F	M	F	M	F	M	F
45–64 years	36	26	33	27	25	26	4	3	26	24	21	24
65–74 years	42	44	67	73	43	43	55	47	47	46	49	39
75 years +	22	30	*	*	32	31	42	51	27	30	31	37

Note: * Data not available.

Table 6.3   Marital status and sex of retired adults (column per cent)

	AT		D		GR		N		PT		UK	
	M	F	M	F	M	F	M	F	M	F	M	F
Married/ Cohabiting	80	40	81	49	86	54	76	45	84	63	72	49
Separated/ Divorced/ Single	(7)	15	8	14	(3)	7	24	56	4	9	13	10
Widowed	14	46	11	39	11	40	*	*	11	38	15	40

Note: * Data not available.

ment among young people. These policies, relatively recently introduced, have yet to impact on the retired population (Figure 6.1). Retired adults in each country are much less likely than adults as a whole to have completed second level secondary or third level education. This is particularly so in Portugal and Greece, starting from a much lower educational base, but also in the UK where policies to encourage greater participation in second and third level education are relatively recent. Although numbers are too small for firm conclusions to be reached, further analysis has suggested that retired women are even less well qualified educationally than retired men.

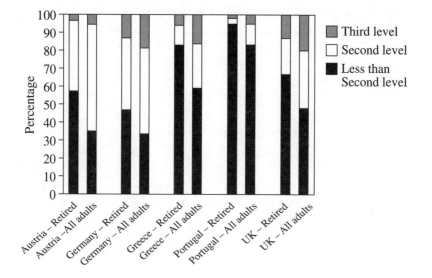

Figure 6.1   Highest educational level of retired adults and all adults

Given their age it is hardly surprising that retired people in each country are approximately two-and-a-half times more likely to be sick and disabled than the adult population as a whole (Figure 6.2).

This picture, with minor exceptions common to each of the study countries, of a large retired population of very elderly, infirm individuals including disproportionate numbers of widowed women has major implications for policies to prevent poverty in retirement. However, there is one further contributory factor to the size of the retired population that has preoccupied governments in recent years – the trend towards early retirement.

EARLY RETIREMENT

The size of the retired population in each country will obviously depend to a large extent on the age at which the state sets official retirement. State Retirement Ages are in the process of being equalised at 65 years for both men and women in each country except Norway, where the SRA for both men and women is 67 years.[1] However in the mid-1990s when the ECHP survey began, official retirement ages varied between men and women in all countries except Norway, with women retiring at 60 in most countries – five years earlier than men. Portuguese men had a state retirement age of 65 years and women of 62 years.

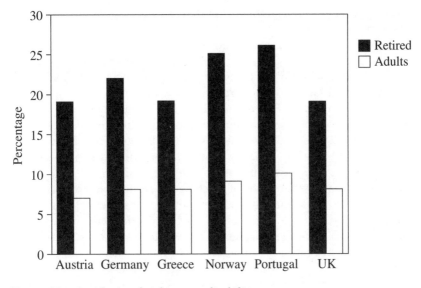

Figure 6.2   Incidence of sickness or disability

Workers in each country are able to take early retirement because of one or a combination of the following factors:

1. statutory provision for workers in particular sectors;
2. statutory provision for the long-term unemployed;
3. statutory provision for long-term sick or disabled;
4. negotiated agreements between workers and employers; and
5. private agreements between workers and employers.

Some countries make statutory provision for certain groups of workers to take earlier retirement with a pension. Greece, for example, allows early retirement at age 55 or 60 years for workers in demanding physical jobs, such as miners, and farmers have been particularly encouraged to take early retirement in the interests of agricultural efficiency. All civil servants in Portugal and many in the UK are entitled to retire at 60 years of age. Some countries allow early retirement for older people who are long-term unemployed. Until 1992, for example, older long-term unemployed workers in Germany could retire at 60 years of age. In the UK, unemployed people over the age of 55 years are not required to be available for and actively seeking work as a condition of benefit receipt. Increasing numbers of people in the UK who are not old enough to receive the state pension have claimed Invalidity Benefit or its replacement, Incapacity Benefit. In Austria an early pension on the grounds of partial disability can be granted to men at the age of 57 years.

Early retirement can also be negotiated between employers and employees. The relatively high state retirement age in Norway has been resisted by workers and, in addition to many workers taking early retirement on the grounds of disability, two-thirds are now covered by the General Agreement on Early Retirement. This has been negotiated between employers and employees and allows workers to retire at 62 years of age. In the UK, negotiated early retirement tends to be on a sectoral basis. For example, until relatively recently teachers were entitled to request early retirement from the age of 50 years.

Workers also have the option of reaching private arrangements with their employers. In the UK and Portugal, for example, it is sometimes in the interests of employers to allow workers to take early retirement and early pensions. The employer can reduce labour costs, either by replacing the workers with younger, less expensive employees or by not replacing them at all.

Provision for a gradual transition into retirement is rare. In most countries workers are either workers or completely retired. Only in Germany and Portugal are workers allowed some statutory flexibility in early retirement with pension entitlement. Since 1996 German workers can take partial retirement at the age of 55 years. If their job is shared with someone who is unemployed or a trainee, the Employment Office will pay a part of the additional cost to the employer. Portuguese workers can also reduce or suspend their employment at the age of 55 years by agreement with their employer. The workers must continue to receive 25 per cent of their wages.

The effects of this can be seen in the large proportions of both men and women aged between 55 and 64 years who are retired in each country except Norway (Table 6.4). For many women, of course, this will mean that they have retired at the (earlier) State Retirement Age and, as a result, more 55–64 year old women than men in each country are retired. However, significant proportions of men in this age group in each country are also retired. Early retirement is particularly prevalent among men in Austria where 58 per cent of men in the 55–64 year age group are retired compared with less than one-third in Portugal and the UK. The differences between retirement rates for men and women in this age group are relatively small for retired Austrians and extremely large for retired men and women in the UK. Over one-half of 55–64 year old women in the UK are retired compared with less than three in ten men.

It is clear that governments in a number of countries have either actively encouraged early retirement, or turned a blind eye to it, in order to reduce the unemployment figures for older workers and/or to improve the employment prospects of the young unemployed. This has been achieved either

Table 6.4   Incidence of retirement among adults over 45 years (cell per cent*)

	AT		D		GR		N		PT		UK	
	M	F	M	F	M	F	M	F	M	F	M	F
45–54 years	(4)	(4)	(4)	*	(4)	(6)	0	0	7	(5)	(4)	(4)
55–64 years	58	63	41	49	41	54	5	5	29	37	29	51
65–74 years	99	100	98	100	90	98	84	85	77	93	96	99
75 years and older	99	100	–	–	99	99	97	99	93	97	98	100

Note: * Table reads proportion of men and women in each age group who are retired.

through statutory provision, or by ignoring the use of invalidity and disability benefits as a 'back door' means of early retirement for the long-term unemployed. The implications have been considered to be so serious in terms of the effects on public expenditure and the loss of workers from the economy that governments have felt obliged to change direction. As a result, governments have introduced:

1.   restrictions on early retirement (for example, among teachers in the UK and long-term unemployed in Germany);
2.   tighter eligibility criteria for early retirement, (raising of the minimum age of eligibility for an early old age pension on the grounds of disability in Austria; tightening of criteria for eligibility to disability pension in Norway and to invalidity-based benefits in the UK); and
3.   special programmes to assist the older long-term unemployed into work (wage subsidies to employers in Austria).

PROVISION IN RETIREMENT

All countries operate a form of compulsory insurance-based pension scheme supplemented by some combination of state provided additional pension, social assistance and private pension arrangements. With the exception of Greece and Austria, all the compulsory insurance-based schemes are administered by the state. Greece's system is administered mainly by a number of sector-based organisations. Austria's scheme is administered by seven institutions, each representing a different professional group. Greece, Austria and Portugal also have separate, more favourable schemes for civil servants.

The design of compulsory state schemes at first sight seems to reflect the priorities of the welfare regimes within each country. Austria and Germany, with their strong corporatist traditions, have schemes which replicate earning patterns during working life in retirement – the more you have earned, the higher your pension. There is no attempt at redistribution from rich to poor and the private pensions sector is relatively underdeveloped.

Norway's social democratic regime overtly aims to redistribute income through the pension system and to provide a minimum pension independent of previous earnings. The aim is to provide a pension for everyone equal to two-thirds of average wages. The scheme also has the apparently contradictory aim of securing income in retirement related to previous earnings. However, the level of income that can be secured is restricted to 12 times the income level that entitles people to the National Insurance basic pension. As a result, and contrary to the expectations of policy makers, occupationally based pension schemes continue to grow in Norway as people attempt to boost further their retirement incomes.

The Portuguese and Greek systems have similar, if more complex, mechanisms to Norway for limiting maximum pensions. Private arrangements are limited although their popularity is growing, particularly among younger professional workers.

The UK system is superficially the most egalitarian with a maximum flat-rate pension payable to all who are eligible, varying only according to whether pensioners are single or living as a couple. However, the value of the pension is low and has declined in recent years relative to wages. All employees must have either an occupational or private pension or, at the time these data were collected, contribute to the State Earnings Related Pension Scheme (SERPS). The benefits from SERPS are likely to be low, providing only up to 20 per cent of average earnings during the whole of the working life. The government has encouraged the growth of occupational and private schemes through tax concessions and other interventions so that a majority of current employees are covered by non-state schemes.

Entitlement to a full state pension in all the countries depends on having made contributions for a certain number of qualifying years, usually approximately 40 years. Calculations of the actual amount of pension payable are complex, involving the number of years of contributions, a percentage of previous income and, as described above, restrictions on the total amount payable in Norway, Greece and Portugal. The UK is the exception with its flat-rate pension for all with adequate contributions' records. Reduced pensions are paid to those with gaps in their contribution records.

Gender and Incomes in Retirement

These pension arrangements, relying as they do on a 40 year history of uninterrupted engagement with the labour market, have major implications for women's incomes in retirement. They are based on a traditional view of family and working life that favours men and, particularly in the 'corporatist' countries, couples in long-term stable marriages. In most countries divorced or separated people are not entitled to a share of their previous partner's pension entitlement. In these systems women are disadvantaged, because their work histories tend to be patchy as a result of child rearing and characterised by shorter periods in work, along with periods of part-time working. Women are also less likely to have occupational or private pensions that might make up for their truncated state contribution record. In retirement many women will, therefore, be dependent on the pensions of their partners for an income. Yet, as we have seen, women are outliving their partners and living on as widows into very old age.

Those without a pension in their own right can have recourse to two main sources of state-provided income in each country: survivors' pensions and the residual benefits system.

Survivors' pensions
Pension systems all recognise the problems which arise for individuals, usually women, when a partner dies and the survivor is not entitled to a pension in their own right. Survivors' pensions are available in each country, although these vary in the proportion of the deceased persons' entitlements which continue to be paid and, in the case of the UK, the age and sex of the survivors. However, the amounts provided in each country are less than the survivor would be entitled to if they could claim a full pension, whether state, occupational or private, in their own right.

Residual systems
In all countries retired people have access to the social assistance system and, in Austria, Greece and Norway, to special schemes designed to secure some form of minimum income specifically for pensioners.

Some of the effect of these provisions on sources of income in retirement can be seen in Table 6.5. In the four countries for which data are available, retired women are far more likely than men to claim to have no income from any source. Presumably most of these women are completely dependent on their spouse or other family members for their livelihood. Women in the UK are far less likely than women in the other countries to claim to have no income from any source.

Women are also less likely than men to say that pensions are their main

Poverty and social exclusion in Europe

Table 6.5   Main source of personal income for retired adults
(cell per cent)

	AT		G*		GR		PT		UK	
	M	F	M	F	M	F	M	F	M	F
No income from any source	*	11	(2)	12	*	19	*	9	*	(3)
Wages and salaries	(5)	(2)	6	(3)	(3)	(1)	(3)	*	(5)	4
Self-employment/farming	*	0	*	*	(3)	(1)	*	*	*	*
Pensions	87	76	84	73	90	68	85	82	76	78
Other social transfers	*	4	*	*	(2)	4	9	6	14	8
Private transfers	*	6	(5)	(4)	(4)	10	*	(2)	(4)	6
Other	*	*	*	8	*	*	*	*	*	*

Note: * Data not available.
        Data for Norway not available.

source of income except in the UK. Women are more likely than men to
have private transfers from other family members outside the household as
their main source of income except in Portugal. A relatively small percentage of retired men and women in each country are dependent on social
transfers as their main source of income, presumably because most will be
in receipt of at least some form of pension, either in their own right or as a
survivor. The largest proportions reliant on other social transfers are in the
UK where the relatively low level of the state retirement pension leaves a
significant proportion of retired people, mainly women, with incomes
below the Income Support (social assistance) threshold.

The Focus of Debate on Pensioner Support

There are two main areas of potential difficulty facing countries in relation
to retirement:

1. the large and increasing proportions of retired people, and the impli-
    cations of this for pensions provision; and
2. the extent of poverty and social exclusion among retired people.

Until relatively recently both policy debates and, particularly, policy
responses have focused almost exclusively on the former of these two problems in each of the study countries. All countries are considering, or have
carried out, reforms aimed at limiting the impact of their ageing populations on public expenditure and containing the effects of the demographic
time bomb. The situation is further complicated in Greece and Portugal by

their relatively undeveloped social security systems and, in Greece, by the need to unify a fragmented system of provision.

At the same time, concern about the current and potential cost of state pensions has led to a range of proposed or actual measures. The systems in Austria, Portugal, Greece and the UK are all undergoing, or have undergone fundamental reviews. Changes in policy under consideration or actually implemented include:

1. Equalisation of pension provision   Pension provision for public sector workers is significantly more generous than for those in the private sector in many countries. In Portugal, for example, the average civil service pension is three-and-a-half to four times higher than for other workers. Proposals to equalise pensions at the lower private sector levels are under consideration in Portugal and Austria.
2. Pension privatisation   Workers are encouraged to provide for their own retirement through taking out occupational and private pensions. This was the route favoured by the UK Government prior to 1997, using the 'carrot' of tax concessions and the 'stick' of eroding the value of state pension provision.
3. Cutting the value of pensions   This can be achieved through adjustments to the basis of calculations for state pensions (under consideration or implemented in Austria, the UK and Portugal); eroding the value of state pensions by linking increases to prices rather than wages (UK); direct cuts in pension provision (under consideration in Greece).
4. Increased targeting and/or means-testing   This involves moving away from the principle of either a universal pension or a pension linked solely to contributions and work history towards a system which provides assistance based on need. This approach is under consideration in Portugal.

In general, therefore, concern with the current and potential cost of pension provision has dominated debate in the study countries to the almost total exclusion of considerations of amelioration of poverty and social exclusion. There are a few exceptions to this. Norway, for example, whilst sharing the concerns of other countries about the possible effects of the demographic time bomb, continues to debate the desirability of increases in state pension provision. The New Labour Government in the UK has introduced a minimum income guarantee for pensioners, albeit set at a relatively low level, but has as yet made no commitment to increasing significantly the level of the state pension or, indeed, of Income Support (social assistance). In the main, however, concern about the potential effects of the demographic time bomb continue to dominate public debate.

The remainder of this chapter attempts to shift this focus by examining the extent of poverty and social exclusion among retired people.

RETIRED PEOPLE, POVERTY AND SOCIAL EXCLUSION

This section describes, first, the extent of income poverty among retired people and characteristics that seem to be particularly associated with poverty, and second, other measures of material deprivation and social exclusion among the elderly are explored.

Income Poverty

Retired people are very much more likely to be poor than adults as a whole in Greece, Portugal and the UK and have similar poverty rates in Austria and Germany. In these two countries it appears that their generous systems of insurance-based pensions are protecting those in retirement from poverty (Table 6.6).

Table 6.6   Income poverty among retired and all adults (cell per cent)

	AT	D	GR	PT	UK
Poverty Rate:					
Retired adults	17	16	35	35	24
All adults	16	16	22	23	17
Poverty Gap:					
Retired adults	4.9	4.8	12.9	10.5	6.2
All adults	5.4	5.0	7.6	7.6	4.3

Notes: Data for Norway not available.

In addition, retired people in Austria and Germany are also protected from severe poverty. When they *are* poor the gap between their incomes and the poverty line is smaller than for poor adults as a whole, as shown by their having a lower 'poverty gap index'. In the UK, Portugal and, in particular, Greece poor retired people experience more severe poverty than poor adults in general.

The extent to which pensions and social transfers combine to keep retired people out of poverty is one way of measuring the effectiveness of systems of financial provision (Table 6.7). Pensions include both state,

*Table 6.7   The role of transfers in preventing poverty among retired people
(cell per cent)*

	AT	D[1]	GR	PT	UK
Retired people:					
Pensions	60	66	42	36	51
Other social transfers	5	–	2	4	19
All adults:					
Pensions	21	22	18	12	15
Other social transfers	8	–	1	5	13

Notes:
Table reads 'additional percentage of retired people who would be in poverty if the social transfer/pension were removed from the household'.
Data for Norway not available.
1. Pension data only is available for Germany.

occupational and private pensions and this should be borne in mind in what follows.

Unsurprisingly, pensions play a much larger role in preventing poverty among retired people than among all adults in each country. Approximately three times more retired people would be in poverty if pensions were removed, except in Greece where the difference is only two-and-a-half times. Pensions are keeping particularly large proportions of retired people out of poverty in Austria and Germany. These countries, as we have seen, have sophisticated and well-developed system of earnings-related pensions and poverty rates are no higher among retired people than among adults as a whole. In the other three countries, where poverty rates are much higher than for all adults, the contribution of pensions to poverty reduction is lower. However in the UK, where the state pension is flat-rate and relatively low, means-tested social transfers play a significant role in keeping retired people out of poverty so that, in total, 70 per cent more retired people would be in poverty if pensions and social transfers were to be removed. Social transfers generally play a larger role in keeping adults out of poverty in the UK than in other countries and their significance is even greater for retired people. Social transfers are generally much less important in the other three countries and, in fact, play a smaller role in poverty reduction among retired people than among the adult population at large.

Regression models aimed at untangling the characteristics that are most likely to be associated with poverty in old age paint a somewhat complex picture. Table 6.8 lists the socio-economic characteristics that are significantly more or less likely to be associated with poverty among

Table 6.8   Factors that prevent or increase poverty among retired people

	Factors that increase poverty	Factors that decrease poverty
AT	SRA to 74 years and 75 years and over (45 years to SRA) Single, never married (Married/cohabiting) Sick and disabled (Not sick or disabled) *Less than second stage secondary education (second stage education)*	Couple with children or 'other' household type (couple no children) Third level education (second stage education)
D	Living alone (couple no children) Less than second stage secondary education (second stage education)	
GR	SRA to 74 years and 75 years and over (45 years to SRA) Living alone (couple no children) Sick and disabled (Not sick or disabled) *Less than second stage secondary education (second stage education)*	*Couple with children*, lone parent with children or *'other' household type* (couple no children) Third level education (second stage education)
PT	SRA to 74 years and 75 years and over (45 years to SRA) Separated/divorced or *single never married (Married/cohabiting)* *Living alone (couple no children)* *Sick and Disabled (not sick and disabled)* *Less than second stage secondary education (second stage education)*	*Couple with children*, lone parent with children *or 'other' household type (couple no children)*
UK	75 years and over (45 years to SRA) *Living alone (couple no children)*	*Single never married (married/cohabiting)* Sick and disabled (not sick and disabled) *Third level education (second stage secondary)*

Note: Data for Norway not available.

retired people in each country. In other words, it shows the circumstances that are most likely to lead to poverty for retired people and those which are most likely to protect retired people from poverty. Characteristics in italics are shared by the adult population as a whole. In other words, having such a characteristic is significantly more likely to be associated with poverty for the adult population as a whole – it is not simply related to retired people. Policies to address poverty caused or prevented by these characteristics need to be aimed at the adult population in general. Those characteristics not in italics are significantly associated with poverty only for retired people and policy interventions might usefully be targeted accordingly.[2] The reference group for each characteristic is shown in parenthesis.

At first sight it seems that retired women are no more likely than retired men to be poor when other characteristics are controlled for. In other words, being retired and female does not significantly increase the risk of being poor of itself. However, retired women tend to be over-represented among those groups of retired people who are seen to have a significantly increased risk of poverty. In particular, being in the age group 75 years and over is significantly associated with a much greater risk of poverty than for the younger retired in each country for which data are available. It has already been seen that women are over-represented in this age group in each country except in Greece.

Analysis not reported here shows that retired people in each country are around two-and-a-half times more likely to be sick and disabled than adults as a whole. Being sick or disabled brings an increased risk of poverty for retired people in all countries except the UK, although in Portugal this is so for adults as a whole, rather than simply for retired people. In the UK retired people who are sick and disabled have a significantly *lower* chance of being poor than those who are in good health. This is probably because of the higher benefits payable to disabled people in the UK. Unaccompanied living also seems to increase the risk of poverty in retirement, whether because people are living alone (Germany, Greece and the UK), or are separated or divorced (Portugal), or are single (Austria and Portugal). However, it seems that being single, never married, helps to protect people from poverty in the UK. In contrast, living in a couple significantly decreases the risk of poverty for retired people in Austria and for all people in Greece and Portugal. Low education qualifications are significantly associated with increased poverty in retirement for all countries except the UK, although this is a characteristic shared by all adults except in Germany. However, having higher level qualifications protects people from poverty in Austria (retired people only), Greece and the UK.

Retired People and Material Deprivation

Patterns of material deprivation are complex (Table 6.9). Levels of each type of deprivation are lowest in Norway[3] and highest in Greece and Portugal, with Germany not far behind. Retired people in each country are slightly more likely than adults as a whole to be deprived of household amenities, presumably because their homes are likely to be older and, therefore, less likely to have modern amenities such as central heating.

In contrast retired people are slightly *less* likely than adults as a whole to be deprived of consumer durables in all countries except Greece. It may be that retired people, being older, have had more time to acquire these items prior to their retirement. The explanation for the Greek figures is unclear. Retired people are also *less* likely to suffer from problems with their housing conditions or in their neighbourhood than adults as a whole, except in Greece and Portugal. However, they are *more* likely to lack household and personal necessities than adults as a whole in all countries except Norway where no-one claims to go without these items.

It seems that material deprivation affects income-poor retired people disproportionately (Table 6.10). In each country income-poor retired people are more likely than the non-income-poor to suffer under each of the four groups of material deprivation. The gaps between the poor and the non-poor tend to be particularly large in Greece and Portugal where income-poor retired people are at least three times more likely to be deprived of household amenities, and at least twice as likely to be deprived of household and personal necessities. The differences between the income poor and non-poor in the other countries, whilst much smaller, are nevertheless noticeable.

It seems, therefore, that whilst levels of material deprivation differ only slightly between retired people and adults as a whole, income poverty among retired people is accompanied by higher levels of material deprivation.

What is most noticeable in this analysis of material deprivation is the similarity between the experiences of retired people in each of the study countries, with the possible exception of Greece and, to a lesser extent, Portugal. Whilst overall, of course, levels of material deprivation differ significantly between the study countries, the experience of material deprivation among retired people relative to the population as a whole, and between income-poor and non-poor retired people in each country, show similar patterns.

Table 6.9 Retired people and material deprivation (cell per cent)

Deprived of:	AT		D		GR		N		PT		UK	
	Retired people	All adults	Retired people	All adults	Retired people	All adults	Retired people	All adults	Retired people	All adults	Retired people	All adults
Household amenities	19	16	25	21	22	16	6	5	32	21	19	15
Consumer durables	17	20	17	23	24	20	1	3	20	21	16	17
Housing/neighbourhood	18	20	13	18	25	20	6	9	25	21	13	19
Household and personal necessities	24	19	19	18	37	23	0	0	32	22	20	18

Table 6.10   *Material deprivation and income poverty among retired people (cell per cent)*

Deprived of:	AT		D		GR		PT		UK	
	Poor	Non-poor	Poor	Non-poor	Poor	Non-poor	Poor	Non-poor	Poor	Non-poor
Household amenities	25	18	38	23	39	12	54	18	26	17
Consumer durables	22	17	21	16	38	17	36	10	21	14
Housing/neighbourhood	(24)	17	(13)	13	31	21	29	23	16	12
Household and personal necessities	33	22	37	15	60	25	49	22	29	17

Note: Data for Norway not available.

Retired People and Social Relationships

One way in which social exclusion can be measured is by the level and nature of social contacts which people have in their every day lives. Poverty and material deprivation can lead to social isolation as people lose touch with neighbours, family and friends. On the other hand, it might be anticipated that retired people would have more social contacts than adults as a whole because of their having more time available without the demands of work.

As with material deprivation, patterns of social contact are complex (Table 6.11). Both retired and non-retired people in Portugal and Greece are far less likely to belong to a club or organisation than people in the other countries. The Norwegians are the most 'clubbable' nationality. However, in each country except the UK retired people are less likely than adults as a whole to be a member of a club or organisation. In contrast retired people in each country, except Greece where levels of contact with neighbours are generally very high, are more likely to have regular contact with their neighbours than are adults in general. Contact with neighbours is generally much higher than club membership, except in Norway where almost two-fifths of retired people and almost half of all adults talk to their neighbours less than once or twice a month.

Patterns of contact with friends and relatives are different again. Austrian, German and Portuguese people have relatively low levels of contact, whilst people in Greece, Norway and the UK are more likely to see relatives and friends on a regular basis. However in each country, and for both the retired and all adults, contact with friends and relatives is lower than with neighbours. Furthermore, retired people in each country except Norway are less likely to have regular contact with friends and relatives than are all adults. This somewhat surprising finding may reflect difficulties in mobility for retired people. It may be easier to keep in contact with neighbours who are, by definition, close by and easily accessible, than with relatives and friends who may live some distance away.

Patterns of social contact for the income-poor and non-poor differ only slightly between retired people and all adults in each country, reflecting the overall trends described above (Table 6.12). However, some differences between income-poor and non-poor retired people do emerge. Poor retired people are less likely than the non-poor to belong to a club or organisation in each country. Poor retired people are slightly more likely to have regular contact with neighbours than non-poor retired in Austria, Norway, Greece and Portugal, slightly less likely in Germany and there are no differences in the UK. Poor retired people are slightly less likely to be in regular contact with friends and relatives than the non-poor retired in each country except Norway and the UK where the reverse is true.

Table 6.11 Retired people and social relationships (cell per cent)

	AT		D		GR		N		PT		UK	
	Retired people	All adults	Retired people	All adults	Retired people	All adults	Retired people	All adults	Retired people	All adults	Retired people	All adults
Not a member of a club/organisation	63	58	54	50	94	91	25	19	90	85	54	54
Talks to neighbours less than once or twice a month	16	21	11	17	6	6	39	48	10	12	11	16
Meets friends/relatives less than once or twice a month	42	31	34	28	15	11	17	21	33	29	18	16

Table 6.12 Social relations and income poverty (cell per cent)

	AT		D		GR		N		PT		UK	
	Poor	Non-poor	Poor	Non-poor	Poor	Non-poor	Poor	Non-poor	Poor	Non-poor	Poor	Non-poor
Not a member of a club/organisation:												
Retired people	68	62	60	53	98	93	35	22	96	86	59	51
All adults	63	56	57	48	96	90	33	17	92	82	64	52
Talks to neighbours less than once or twice a month:												
Retired people	16	17	(13)	11	4	6	33	41	8	11	11	11
All adults	24	21	19	17	4	6	48	48	8	13	13	17
Meets friends/relatives less than once or twice a month:												
Retired people	43	41	40	33	15	14	13	18	38	31	16	18
All adults	33	31	31	27	13	11	15	21	33	27	15	16

It seems, therefore, that in general retired people are slightly more likely to be socially isolated than adults as a whole. Although they are more likely to have regular contacts with neighbours, they are less likely to belong to clubs or other organisations and less likely to see friends and relatives on a regular basis. These trends are more pronounced among income-poor retired people.

CONCLUSION

The nature and extent of pension provision in our study countries varies significantly, broadly according to Esping-Andersen's typology of contrasting welfare regimes. The outcomes for pensioners in terms of income poverty reflect these differing regimes. Retired people in Austria and Germany experience levels of poverty no higher than for the population as a whole and their poverty is no more severe. Rates and severity of poverty among retired people in Greece and Portugal are much higher than for the population as a whole. The UK comes somewhere in between.

However, these apparent differences conceal similarities in the characteristics of poor retired people across countries. In each country except Germany (for whom this age group cannot be analysed separately) being old and, in particular, being aged 75 years and over brings a significantly higher risk of poverty when all other characteristics are controlled for. In other words, the older you are the more likely you are to be poor. Our analysis has shown that between one-quarter and one-half of retired people in each country are aged 75 years and over and these proportions can only be expected to increase with increasing life expectancy. Living alone also significantly increases the risk of poverty in each of our study countries. Women are over-represented among the oldest groups of retired people in each country except Greece, and are more likely to live alone. They therefore form a disproportionately large share of the poor retired population.

The question remains as to whether current policy responses can provide the answer to poverty in old age, particularly among women. Discouraging early retirement can have only a limited effect since, as has been shown, poverty rates are much higher among the older age groups. People taking early retirement tend to be those who are better provided for in pension terms, mainly men, and are less likely to join the ranks of the income poor. Encouraging individuals to make their own additional pension arrangements outside of the state system will benefit most those individuals who have regular, well-paid participation in the labour market over lengthy periods. It might be anticipated that, as women's participation in the labour market increases, their entitlement to pensions in their own right would increase. However, the numbers of previously partnered women who have incomplete pension contribution records in their own right, whether state or private, are likely to increase. This, combined with the part-time, intermittent nature of women's work and their lower wages, means that women's incomes in retirement are likely to continue to be lower than men's. In Norway, despite the projected increase in pensioner income for both men and women, women's incomes are expected to grow by a smaller amount than men's so that the gap will increase. This is because disproportionate numbers of men have private pensions, incomes from which are anticipated to grow at a faster rate than state pension provision on which more women will continue to depend. Women workers in the UK are also less likely than men to be members of a private or occupational pension scheme, despite government emphasis on this type of provision. Only just over half as many women as men were paying into an occupational pension scheme in 1991, and even among full-time workers women were less likely than men to have an additional pension. Even when women do have an occupational pension their income from these is smaller than men's. For example, women in the UK aged 65 to 69 years who have occupational pensions receive an income only one-third as high as men's.

Finally there is the option of cutting the value of state pensions. This can only increase impoverishment among those who are already most vulnerable to poverty. Whilst it may help national exchequers to limit social security expenditures, the direct cost in terms of increased reliance on social assistance and the indirect costs of more ill-health, for example, might in the long run prove counterproductive.

To date national governments have been almost exclusively concerned in policy terms with the cost of pension provision and have almost totally neglected the policy problem of how to reduce poverty in old age, particularly among women. Whilst the extent of poverty in old age varies from country to country, those who experience it are the same – the oldest and those living alone.

NOTES

1. Strictly speaking the UK does not have an official state retirement age but a state pension age, that is, the age at which men and women become eligible for the state retirement pension.
2. Significant at the 0.05 level.
3. However, it should be noted that in Norway questions about lacking household and personal necessities were only asked of those respondents who claimed to be having difficulties making ends meet. Nevertheless, this might have been anticipated to have led to higher levels of deprivation rather than these very low levels.

7. Patterns of social exclusion: implications for policy and research

Christopher Heady and Graham Room

The purpose of this chapter is to bring together the analysis in the preceding chapters by summarising the main results, discussing their implications for the European policy agenda and indicating areas for further data collection and analysis.

As explained in Chapter 1, the book has three objectives: to increase understanding of poverty and disadvantage, to examine and compare the extent and impact of such deprivation, and to establish the effect of government policies on these phenomena.

The research described in the preceding chapters fulfils these objectives by looking at the problems of poverty and social exclusion from the point of view of four 'risk groups': young adults, lone parents, sick and disabled people, and the retired. In the context of information on the broad characteristics of these groups and the policies towards them in each country, ECHP data (except for Norway) are used to compare the incidence of poverty and non-monetary deprivation of people in these groups with the rest of the population. This is to identify the factors that increase or reduce the risk of deprivation for members of each group, and to identify the impact of social transfers received by members of each group.

THE ROLES OF FAMILIES, EMPLOYMENT AND SOCIAL POLICY

The results in the risk group chapters show considerable complexity. The characteristics of the risk groups, particularly young adults and lone parents, are different in each country. This means that the differences in observed deprivation do not only reflect differences in policy. Also, there is a remarkably low correlation, among individuals, between poverty and non-monetary deprivation. However, there are still some interesting patterns that emerge.

First, only two of the risk groups have a higher incidence of poverty than the general population in all six countries: lone parents and the sick and disabled. The poverty rate is higher for the retired in all countries apart from Austria and Germany (data for Norway were not available). In contrast, the poverty rate of young people is only higher than that of all adults in Germany and Norway. The last of these findings is particularly interesting as much policy discussion does identify young people as being at risk of social exclusion because of their less secure attachment to the labour market (which is confirmed in the data).

Second, comparing countries, Austria has relatively low poverty rates for all risk groups and Greece and Portugal are not amongst the countries with relatively low poverty rates for any of the risk groups. However, the other three countries show no consistency. Germany has relatively high poverty rates for young adults and lone parents but a relatively low rate for the retired. Norway has a high poverty rate for young adults but low rates for lone parents and the sick and disabled. The UK has the highest poverty rate for lone parents but the lowest for young adults.

Third, there is considerable consistency in the factors that determine whether members of each risk group are below the poverty line. Employment and high levels of education generally reduce the chances of a person being in poverty. In contrast, living alone and living with dependent children both increase the risk of poverty. For lone parents, the fact that at least one child is dependent increases the poverty rate, but by very different amounts in different countries. Factors such as age, sex and marital status show a less consistent pattern.

Fourth, for the five EU countries social transfers of all types have the greatest proportional effect in reducing poverty amongst the retired, followed by sick and disabled people, young adults and lone parents. However, given the lower incidence of poverty amongst young adults than lone parents, the proportion of lone parents that are taken out of poverty by social transfers is higher than the proportion of young adults. For all risk groups, Austria has the highest proportional reductions in poverty from social transfers while Portugal has the lowest. Germany ranks close to Austria for the retired and sick and disabled people but much lower for lone parents and young adults. Greece does a little better than Portugal for all groups. The UK takes intermediate positions, behind Germany for the retired and the sick and disabled, and above it for young adults and lone parents.

Fifth, as one would expect from the poverty rates, the sick and disabled group and lone parents experience higher rates of non-monetary material deprivation than the population as a whole. Also, the retired experience worse housing conditions and find it more difficult to buy household necessities although they are less likely to lack consumable durables. Despite their generally low poverty rates, young adults are more likely to lack consumer durables. Thus, the relationship between poverty and non-monetary material deprivation is more complex than one might expect. It is particularly interesting that, even when controlling for their poverty, both lone parents and those who are sick and disabled are more likely to experience non-monetary material deprivation than the rest of the population. This suggests that the equivalence scales used in measuring poverty are not reflecting the additional costs of living for members of these two risk groups.

Sixth, the effect of poverty on social relations is mixed and never very strong. Young people are slightly less likely to engage in social activities if they are poor. There are no clear differences between lone parents and partnered parents in their social activities, and there are not enough observations to tell whether poverty makes a difference. Sick and disabled people are less likely to engage in social activities than other adults but there are not enough observations to tell whether this has to do with their state of health or their poverty. Finally, retired people are less likely to join clubs than other adults (except in the UK) but are more likely to have regular contact with neighbours (except Greece), while there is no clear pattern for meeting friends and relatives. Poor retired people are less likely to join clubs and (except for Norway and the UK) meet friends and relatives than the non-poor, but are more likely to have regular contact with neighbours (except for Germany and the UK).

These results have interesting implications for our understanding of poverty and social exclusion. Considering first the determinants of poverty, the role of employment and education in reducing the risk of poverty are well known and understood. However, the international comparison of lone parents emphasises the importance of work by showing that the UK, which has the lowest labour force participation of lone mothers, has the highest level of poverty despite the fact that social transfers are moderately effective. The role of family structures is less commonly discussed, but these results show them to be important. People living alone are at greater risk of poverty because they have no one else to contribute if income is reduced. This is particularly well illustrated in the case of young adults, where high rates of unemployment in some countries do not result in excess poverty rates, presumably because many of the people affected are living with their parents. The importance of family structure is also emphasised by the substantial difference in experience between lone mothers with dependent children and those who only have non-dependent children.

Turning to the effect of government policy on poverty, the fact that a country with high levels of social expenditure, such as in Austria, can achieve low levels of poverty is unsurprising. However, Germany's relative success in protecting retired and sick and disabled people from poverty contrasts with its relative failure to protect young adults and lone parents. This provides a useful reminder of the strengths and weaknesses of an income–maintenance approach to social transfer policy: it protects those with a history of good incomes, but not those without.

Some of the analysis of government policy raises more questions than it answers. Why is it that all six countries fail to reduce the poverty rate among sick and disabled people to that of the general population, especially when this group has living costs that are greater than average? Much of the policy discussion suggests that this may be because of a concern about people misrepresenting themselves as unfit to work, but why not rely on more stringent medical tests? In Greece, Portugal and the UK, retired people are also left with a higher risk of poverty, and here there is no risk of misrepresentation. Is this because retired people do not see their own situation as being bad, presumably because they have lived through harder times, and so do not complain so loudly?

While this analysis of poverty yields valuable insights, it is the link between poverty on the one hand and non-monetary measures of deprivation and social isolation on the other that is really intriguing. After all, it is these latter measures that get closest to what determines peoples' quality of life, even though it is the monetary measure of poverty that is usually most susceptible to government policies. Here we find that poverty has little effect on social isolation, presumably because much social contact is fairly inexpensive and takes place between people at similar income levels. In contrast, there is definitely a link between poverty and non-monetary measures of material deprivation. However, it is not simple. Although the poorest groups are also the most deprived, poor individuals are not necessarily deprived, and hardly ever suffer deprivation in all aspects of their life. Similarly, not all people who are deprived are also poor.

This lack of complete correspondence between poverty and deprivation could perhaps partly be explained by differences between people in how good they are at managing on a limited budget. However, the data suggest that there is more to it than that. For example, the retired are not (on average) more deprived of consumer durables even though they are more frequently poor. In contrast, young adults are more deprived of consumable durables even though they are less frequently poor. One obvious explanation of this is that the poor retired still have their consumer durables that were bought in a time when they were not poor, while the young adults have not yet had time to accumulate them. This is not a complete explanation of the data, for example it does not explain why the retired are so lacking in household amenities, but it provides a reasonable explanation of why there is such a poor correlation between poverty and deprivation. Different people have different histories of income and purchases, and so experience a different effect of current poverty on current deprivation.

Another way of expressing this idea is that deprivation is a dynamic process and so can really only be understood as the result of a history of experiences. It therefore does not fit well into a static comparison with current poverty. As it is this sort of non-monetary material deprivation that is normally regarded as more relevant to the concept of social exclusion than poverty, because it is the lack of these things that might hamper social participation, this view and the data that it seeks to explain support the argument that social exclusion can only be understood as a dynamic process.

EUROPEAN POLICY IMPLICATIONS

The research reported in this book was launched in 1997. During the period since then, the EU has steadily strengthened its commitment to combating social exclusion. The Amsterdam Treaty made the combating of exclusion an explicit objective of the Community (Treaty establishing the European Community, Article 136). The Lisbon Summit of March 2000 set out a new set of strategic goals for the Union, designed to create a knowledge-based economy, but recognising the new risks of social exclusion that this might generate and the consequent imperative for policies to promote social inclusion.

The EU institutions and the member states have recognised that for effective policies to be developed and monitored, an improved understanding of social exclusion is first required. During 2000 the High Level Group on Social Protection was given the task of defining indicators that could then be used as benchmarks for national policies to combat social exclusion. The Nice Summit of December 2000 asked Member States to submit by June 2001 national action plans covering a two-year period, with indicators and monitoring mechanisms capable of measuring progress (Presidency Conclusions, para. 18). The European Commission and the Council have agreed a proposal for a new action programme in this field (COM (2000) 368), a key part of which is to improve understanding. All of these policy initiatives presuppose an improved understanding of poverty and social exclusion, something to which the research reported in this book makes, we believe, a substantial contribution.

As the research underlines, processes of social exclusion are inextricably linked to other economic, social and political developments: for example, changes in employment opportunities and in social protection systems. It is not only national and EU policies in the field of social exclusion that are relevant. It is therefore significant that the mid- and late-1990s saw substantial moves towards concerted European action in the field of employment policy and an intensified debate on the modernisation of social protection systems. The research findings in this book are relevant to both.

Indebted to the Delors White Paper on Growth, Competitiveness and Employment of 1993, the Essen Summit of 1994, and the Luxembourg Employment Summit of Autumn 1997 established the framework for concerted action under four pillars: employability, adaptability, entrepreneurship and equal opportunities. This framework has subsequently become the basis for an annual cycle of national reporting and multilateral benchmarking. Our research findings illuminate the implications of two of these pillars in particular for measures to combat social exclusion: employability and equal opportunities.

'Employability' includes reference to the transition from school to work, training and lifelong learning. Our research findings similarly give a central place to education and training, and human resource policies in the workplace, as a means of securing the social integration of young people in particular. However, they also highlight the barriers to education and training that are posed by governmental attempts to impose a growing proportion of the costs onto the individuals concerned.

'Equal opportunities' includes measures to reconcile work and family life, something of particular importance for lone mothers. Our findings confirm that employment (along with re-partnering) is one of the best protections against poverty for lone parents, with the availability of childcare facilities crucial to enabling them to take advantage of employment opportunities.

The modernisation of social protection systems has been a further area of concerted debate, if not action, at EU level. These systems grew piecemeal in response to industrialisation at a time when individuals' lives tended to be static geographically, relationally and economically. In contrast, all these aspects of life in a post-modern society are characterised by rapid change. Our findings confirm the importance of social transfer payments in reducing levels of poverty among elderly and sick people in particular. These are the 'traditional' targets of social protection systems. However, our findings are also consistent with the argument that traditional social protection systems deal less effectively with those groups of the population whose vulnerability is a feature of recent decades – young people and lone parents.

Two Communications from the European Commission, relating to social protection, have appeared during the period of this project: the 1997 Communication, *Modernising and Improving Social Protection in the European Union,* and the 1999 Communication, *A Concerted Strategy for Modernising Social Protection.* Among the issues upon which these Communications focus are three in particular to which our research findings are relevant.

The first is the individualisation of social rights, with particular reference to women, so that their social protection is no longer subsidiary to that of a male breadwinner, especially given the precarious nature of modern family relationships. As our findings confirm, poverty and deprivation affect women disproportionately: especially lone mothers and female pensioners. As is increasingly recognised, their social insurance contribution records, commonly less complete than their male counterparts when earnings are interrupted, because of caring and home management responsibilities, can no longer be assumed to be cushioned by those of a partner.

The second is the combining of minimum income benefits with active pathways to enable reintegration into the labour market, as part of a wider strategy to make social protection more employment-friendly. As our findings confirm, full-time employment provides the best protection against poverty. However, much low-paid work remains, and in some countries there is growing polarisation between work-rich and work-poor households. Making social protection more employment-friendly may therefore not suffice as a strategy for promoting social inclusion, even among those of working age.

The third issue in these Communications to which our research is relevant concerns measures to secure the sustainability of public pension schemes, as part of the effort to adapt social protection to the demographic ageing of the population. Our findings underline that while poverty among older people is in general less severe than it was a generation ago, they continue to enjoy a substantially lower standard of living than the rest of the population, notably in the southern countries and the UK. Poverty among the elderly has by no means been abolished. Moreover, during the coming decades, new cohorts of pensioners will include substantial numbers of people with contribution records which have been interrupted by the high unemployment of recent decades; at the same time, we must expect growing political resistance by those of working age to supporting an expanding pensioner generation. The sustainability of public pension schemes in face of this twin challenge must be in doubt; worsening poverty among such pensioners the growing risk.

IMPLICATIONS FOR DATA INSTRUMENTS AND RESEARCH

The European Community Household Panel, the basis for the empirical data that this study analyses, was launched in the early 1990s. Its purpose was to provide policy researchers, statistical offices and policy makers with tools for monitoring the social and economic conditions of households and for analysing how these developed over time. This purpose would, uniquely, be served by developing a data instrument common across most of the countries of the EU enabling, on the one hand, rigorous comparative study of household trajectories and the effectiveness of national policies and, on the other, the regular production of data concerning the social conditions of the EU population as a whole. Monitoring and analysing risks of social exclusion were to be a central and explicit part of this task.

How far have the ECHP data enabled us to analyse patterns and dynamics of social exclusion? What implications follow from our work for the data instruments of this sort that could be developed at EU level?

The research reported in this book has consisted primarily of the analysis of cross-sectional data, in international comparison. As discussed above, it has produced some interesting new insights into the determinants of poverty and social deprivation, including the roles of family structures and government policy. However, it has been limited by the small sample sizes of the surveys that the ECHP uses, which has prevented a more detailed breakdown of the risk groups into sub-groups that face different circumstances. More detailed work, of broadly the same type, would be of value but must await the development of larger datasets.

Another direction in which this research could be developed is by the use of panel data over a longer period, which has the potential to analyse the dynamics of the process of social exclusion. It also allows the resolution of certain statistical problems, such as controlling for unobserved differences between individuals. The power of such analysis has been demonstrated by many of the studies that have used well-established panel data from such countries as the United States, Germany, Sweden and the UK. However, these panel datasets are not designed to be internationally comparable and do not cover such a wide range of countries as those covered in this book. It is, therefore, to future waves of the ECHP that we must look for a dynamic extension of the work reported here. A second book based on this research will begin such a dynamic analysis.

The content of the datasets is obviously also important, not just their size and the period over which they are collected. Our work allows us to comment on the relative wealth and poverty of the ECHP for tapping different variables relevant to the analysis of social exclusion. The ECHP provides a useful array of data concerned with social benefits and employment. However, the questions dealing with social relationships are rather sparse: this is somewhat surprising, given that these relational aspects of social exclusion are central to the debates from which the ECHP, in part, sprang (Room, 1995b). The questions concerned with people's experience of education and training are also rather limited: again, this is rather surprising, given the general acknowledgement in European policy debates of the importance of education and training for securing the reinsertion of those at risk of marginalisation. The role of parents in supporting their children's educational and employment development appears to be crucial, but the ECHP provides little information on the extent to which parents contribute (directly or indirectly) to the costs of education for post-school leaving age children and on the constraints that people face in accessing education and training.

Much current theorising about social exclusion goes beyond the individual and the household, to deal with neighbourhood effects, in terms of crime levels, poor housing condition, poor schools and low employment opportunities. Within individual countries of the EU there are a variety of studies and policy indicators, concerned with conceptualising and measuring deprivation and exclusion at the level but of the local community, not of the household (Robson, 1995; Aldeghi, 1995; DETR, 2000). There are also surveys in developing countries that report characteristics of neighbourhoods, such as the Living Standards Measurement Surveys that have been promoted by the World Bank. However, such data are not available in the ECHP or in other surveys conducted on a systematic and comparative basis in European countries. Methodologically this may, indeed, be the greatest challenge to come out of our work: how to combine the insights which can be drawn from panel studies of households with information concerning the communities and institutions in which they live, and with reference to which their social inclusion and exclusion must ultimately be judged.

References

Aldeghi, I. (1995), 'Measuring Socioeconomic Differences within Areas: the French analysis', in G. Room (ed.), *Beyond the Threshold: The Measurement and Analysis of Social Exclusion*, Bristol: The Policy Press.

Amera, A. (1996), 'Chronically Disabled and Social Exclusion', in Ekke (ed.), *Dimensions of Social Exclusion: Main Issues and Identification of Policy Priorities*, Athens: National Institute for Social Research, 55–76.

Atkinson, A.B. (1991), 'Comparing poverty rates internationally: Lessons from recent studies in developed countries', *World Bank Economic Review*, **5**, 3–21.

Atkinson, A.B. (1998), 'Social Exclusion, Poverty and Unemployment', in A.B. Atkinson and J. Hills (eds), *Exclusion, Employment and Opportunity*, CASEpaper 4, London: Centre for Analysis of Social Exclusion.

Atkinson, A.B., Rainwater, M. and Smeedling, T. (1995), *Income Distribution in OECD Countries*, Paris: OECD.

Bane, M.J. and Ellwood, D.T. (1986), 'Slipping in and out of poverty: the dynamics of spells', *Journal of Human Resources*, **21**(1), 1–23.

Berghman, J. (1995), 'Social Exclusion in Europe: Policy Context and Analytical Framework', in G. Room (ed.), *Beyond the Threshold: The Measurement and Analysis of Social Exclusion*, Bristol: The Policy Press.

Berthoud, R., Lakey, J. and McKay, S. (1993), *The Economic Problems of Disabled People*, London: Policy Studies Institute.

Bradshaw, J., Kennedy, S., Kilkey, M., Hutton, S., Corden, A. Eardley, T., Holmes, H. and Neale, J. (1996), *The Employment of Lone Parents: a Comparison of Policy in 20 Countries*, London: Family Policy Studies Centre.

Bruce, B. and Jäntti, M. (2001), 'Child poverty across the industrialised world: evidence from the Luxembourg Income Study', in Koen, V. and Smeeding T.M. (eds), *Child Wellbeing, Child Poverty and Child Policy in Modern Nations*, Bristol: The Policy Press, 11–32.

Buhmann, B., Rainwater, L., Schmaus, G. and Smeeding, T. (1988), 'Equivalence scales, well-being, inequality and poverty: Estimates across ten countries using the LIS database', *Review of Income and Wealth*, **34**, 115–42.

Burchardt, T., Le Grand, J. and Piachaud, D. (1999), 'Social exclusion in Britain 1991–1995', *Social Policy and Administration*, **33**(3), September.

Callan, T., Nolan, B. and Whelan, C.T. (1993), 'Concepts of poverty and the poverty line: a critical survey of approaches to measure poverty', *Journal of Economic Surveys*, **5**, 243–62.

Chaudhuri, S. and Ravallion, M. (1994), 'How well do static indicators identify the chronically poor?', *Journal of Public Economics*, **53**, 367–94.

Christopher, K., England, P., McLanahan, S., Ross, K. and Smeeding, T. (2001), 'Gender inequality in poverty in affluent nations: the role of single motherhood and the state', in Vleminchx, K. and Smeeding, T.S. (eds), *Child Well-Being, Child Poverty and Child Policy in Modern Nations*, Bristol: The Policy Press.

Department for Environment, Transport and the Regions (DETR) (2000), *Measuring Multiple Deprivation at the Small Area Level*, London.

Department of Social Security (DSS) (1999a), *Opportunity for All: Tackling Poverty and Social Exclusion*, Cm 445, London: HMSO.

Ditch, J., Barnes, H., Bradshaw, J. and Kilkey, M. (1996), *A Synthesis of National Family Policies in 1996*, Brussels: European Observatory on National Family Policies.

Duncan, S. and Edwards, R. (1999), *Lone Mothers, Paid Work and Gendered Moral Rationalities*, Macmillan: Basingstoke.

Eardley, T., Bradshaw, J., Ditch, J., Gough, I. and Whiteford, P. (1996), *Social Assistance Schemes in OECD Countries*, Department of Social Security Research Report 46, London: HMSO.

Esping-Andersen, G. (1990), *The Three Worlds of Welfare Capitalism*, Oxford: Polity Press and Blackwell.

European Commission (1984), Council Decision of December 19, 1984.

European Commission (1993), *White Paper on Growth, Competitiveness and Employment*, Luxembourg.

European Commission (1997), Communication, *Modernising and Improving Social Protection in the European Union* (COM(97)102), Brussels.

European Commission (1999), Communication, *A Concerted Strategy for Modernising Social Protection*, Brussels.

European Commission (2000), *Decision Establishing a Community Action to Encourage Cooperation between Member States to Combat Social Exclusion* (COM(2000)368), Brussels.

Eurostat (1990) *Poverty in Figures – Europe in the early 1980s*, Theme 3, Series C, Luxembourg: OPOCE.

Eurostat (1994) *Poverty Statistics in the late 1980s – Research based on Microdata*, Theme 3, Series C, Luxembourg: OPOCE.

Eurostat (1997) *Statistics in Focus*, Theme 2 'Population and social conditions', Series 6, Luxembourg: OPOCE.

Eurostat (2000), *European Social Statistics: Income, Poverty and Social Exclusion*, 2000 Edition, Luxembourg: Office for Official Publications of the European Communities.

Forssén, K. (1998), *Child Poverty and Family Policy in the OECD Countries*, Luxembourg Income Study Working Papers, No. 178, Luxembourg:

Foster, J.E., Greer, J. and Thorbecke, E. (1984), 'A class of decomposable poverty measures', *Econometrica*, **52**, 761–6.

Gallie, D. and Paugum, S. (2000), (eds), *Welfare Regimes and the Experience of Unemployment*, Oxford: Oxford University Press.

Goodin, R.E. Headey, B., Muffels, R. and Dirven, H.-J. (1999), *The Real Worlds of Welfare Capitalism*, Cambridge: Cambridge University Press.

Hagenaars, A.J.M., de Vos, K. and Zaidi, M.A. (1994), *Poverty Statistics in the late 1980s: Research Based on Micro-data*, Theme 3, Series C, Luxembourg: Eurostat.

Hallerod, B. (1995), 'The truly poor: Direct and indirect consensual measurement of poverty in Sweden', *Journal of European Social Policy*, **5**, 111–29.

Haveman, R. (1990), 'Poverty statistics in the European Community: assessment and recommendations', in R. Teekens and B.S.M. van Praag (eds), *Analysing Poverty in the European Community*, Eurostat News special edition, Luxembourg: Eurostat, 459–67.

Heady, C., Mitrakos, Th. and Tsakloglou, P. (1999), 'The distributional impact of social transfers in the EU: Evidence from the ECHP', Athens University of Economics and Business, Department of International and European Economic Studies Discussion Paper No. 99-04.

Hobson, B. (1994), 'Solo Mothers, Social Policy Regimes and the Logics of Gender', in D. Sainsbury (ed.), *Gendering Welfare States*, London: Sage.

Immervoll, H., Sutherland, H. and de Vos, K. (2000), 'Child poverty and child benefits in the European Union', EUROMOD Working Paper EM1/00, Microsimulation Unit, Department of Applied Economics, University of Cambridge.

ISSAS (1990), *Poverty in Figures: Europe in the Early 1980s*, Theme 3, Series C, Luxembourg: Eurostat.

Johnson, D.S. and Garner, T.I. (1995), 'Unique equivalence scales: Estimation and implications for distributional analysis', *Journal of Income Distribution*, **4**, 215–34.

Kilkey, M. and Bradshaw, J. (1999), 'Lone Mothers, Economic Well-being and Policies', in D. Sainsbury (ed.), *Gender and Welfare state regimes*, Oxford: Oxford University Press.

Lee, P. and Murie, A. (1999), *Literature Review on Social Exclusion*, Edinburgh: The Scottish Office Central Research Unit.

Leira, A. (1992), *Welfare States and Working Mothers: the Scandinavian Experience*, Cambridge: Cambridge University Press.

Leisering, L. and Walker, R. (1998), *The Dynamics of Modern Society: Poverty, Policy and Welfare*, Bristol: The Policy Press.

Lessof, C. and Jowell, R. (1999), 'Measuring social exclusion', *Social Exclusion Statistics*, conference paper, Esher: Imac Research.

Levitas, R. (1998), *The Inclusive Society? Social Exclusion and New Labour*, Basingstoke: Macmillan.

Lewis, J. (1997), *Lone Mothers in European Welfare Regimes*, London: Jessica Kingsley Press.

Mack, J. and Lansley, S. (1985), *Poor Britain*, London: Allen and Unwin.

Mejer, L. (1999), 'The E.U. methodological approach', *Social Exclusion Statistics*, conference paper, Esher: Imac Research.

Millar, J. (1994), 'Defining Lone Parenthood: Family Structures and Social Relations', in L. Hantrais and M.T. Letablier (eds), *Conceptualising the Family*, University of Loughborough: Cross National Research Papers.

Millar, J. (1996), 'Mothers, Workers, Wives; Comparing policy approaches to supporting lone parents', in E. Bortolaia Silva (ed.), *Good Enough Mothering? Feminist perspectives on on lone motherhood*, London: Routledge.

Millar, J. (2000), 'Genere, povert e esclusione sociale', in Bimbi, F. and Ruspini, E. (eds), Povert delle donne e trasformazione dei rapporti di genere, Inciesta, 128, aprile-giugno 2000, 9–13.

Millar, J. (2001), 'Benefits for children in the UK', in K. Battle and M. Mendelson (eds), *Benefits for Children: A four country study*, Canada: Caledon Institute.

Millar, J. and Warman, A. (1996), *Family Obligations in Europe*, London: Family Policy Studies Centre.

Millar, J. and Rowlingson, R. (2001) (eds), *Lone Parents, Employment and Social Policy*, Bristol: The Policy Press.

Muffels, R., Berghman, J. and Dirven, H.-J. (1992), 'A multi-method approach to monitoring the evolution of poverty', *Journal of European Social Policy*, **2**, 193–213.

Nolan, B. and Whelan, C.T. (1996), 'Measuring poverty using income and deprivation indicators: Alternative approaches', *Journal of European Social Policy*, **6**, 225–40.

Nolan, B., Whelan, C.T., Layte, R. and Maitre, B. (1999), *Income, Deprivation and Economic Strain: An Analysis of the European Community Household Panel*, Dublin: The Economic and Social Research Institute.

O'Higgins, M. and Jenkins, S. (1990), 'Poverty in EC: Estimates for 1975,

1980 and 1985', in R. Teekens and B.M.S. van Praag (eds), *Analysing Poverty in the European Community*, Eurostat News Special Edition, Luxembourg: Eurostat.

Paugam, S. (1995), 'The Spiral of Precariousness: A multi-dimensional approach to the process of social disqualification in France', in G. Room (ed.), *Beyond the Threshold: The Measurement and Analysis of Social Exclusion*, Bristol: The Policy Press.

Paugam, S. (1996), 'Poverty and social disqualification: a comparative analysis of cumulative disadvantage in Europe', *Journal of European Social Policy*, **6** (4), 287–304.

Piachaud, D. (1981), 'Peter Townsend and the Holy Grail', *New Society*, 10 September, 419–21.

Ramprakash, D. (1994), 'Poverty in the countries of the European Union: A synthesis of Eurostat's statistical research on poverty', *Journal of European Social Policy*, **4** (2), 117–28.

Ringen, S. (1985), 'Toward a third stage in the measurement of poverty', *Acta Sociologica*, **28**, 99–113.

Ringen, S. (1988), 'Direct and indirect measures of poverty', *Journal of Social Policy*, **17**, 351–66.

Robson, B. (1995), 'The Development of the 1991 Local Deprivation Index', in G. Room (ed.) (1995), *Beyond the Threshold: The Measurement and Analysis of Social Exclusion*, Bristol: The Policy Press.

Rodrigues, C.F. (1999), 'Income distribution and poverty in Portugal: 1994/95', Technical University of Lisbon, Department of Economics Discussion Paper 4/1999.

Roll, J. (1992), *Lone-parent Families in the European Community*, London: Family Policy Studies Centre.

Room, G. (ed.) (1995a), *Beyond the Threshold: The Measurement and Analysis of Social Exclusion*, Bristol: The Policy Press.

Room, G. (1995b), 'Poverty in Europe: competing paradigms of analysis', *Policy and Politics*, **23** (2), 103–13.

Room, G. (1999), 'Social exclusion, solidarity and the challenge of globalisation', *International Journal of Social Welfare*, **8** (3), 166–74.

Rowntree, S. (1901), *Poverty: A Study of Town Life*, London: Nelson.

Rowntree, B.S. (1941), *Poverty and Progress*, London: Longmans Green, 102.

Schaber, G., Schmaus, G. and Wagner, G. (1993), *The PACO Project*, Luxembourg: CEPS/INSTEAD.

Sen, A.K. (1976), 'Poverty: An ordinal approach to measurement', *Econometrica*, **44**, 219–31.

Sen, A.K. (1983), 'Poor, relatively speaking', *Oxford Economic Papers*, **35**, 153–69.

Sen, A.K. (1985), 'A sociological approach to the measurement of poverty: A reply to Professor Peter Townsend', *Oxford Economic Papers*, **37**, 669–76.

Sen, A.K. (1992), *Inequality reexamined*, Oxford: Clarendon Press.

Skevik, A. (1999), 'Mothers, carers, wives and workers: lone mothers in Norwegian social policy', in D. Bouget and B. Palier (eds), *Comparing Social Welfare Systems in Nordic Europe and France*, Paris: MIRE.

Skevik, A. (2001), 'Lone parents and employment in Norway' in J. Millar and K. Rowlingson (eds), *Lone Parents and Employment: Cross-national Perspectives*, Bristol: The Policy Press.

Smeeding, T.M., Saunders, P., Coder, J., Jenkins, S., Fritzell, J. Hagenaars, A.J.M., Hauser, R. and Wolfson, M. (1993), 'Poverty, inequality and living standard impacts across seven nations: the effects of non-cash subsidies for health, education and housing', *Review of Income and Wealth*, **39**, 229–56.

Townsend, P. (1979), *Poverty in the UK*, Penguin.

Townsend, P. (1985), 'A sociological approach to the measurement of poverty – A rejoinder to Professor Amartya Sen', *Oxford Economic Papers*, **37**, 659–68.

Tsakloglou, P. (1996), 'Elderly and non-elderly in the European Union: A comparison of living standards', *Review of Income and Wealth*, **42**, 271–91.

Tsakloglou, P. (1998), *Poverty, Social Exclusion, Multi-dimensional Disadvantage and Mobility in Six European Countries*, Department of International and European Economic Studies, Athens University of Economics and Business.

Tsakloglou, P. and Panopoulou, G. (1998), 'Who are the poor in Greece?: Analysing poverty under alternative concepts of resources and equivalence scales', *Journal of European Social Policy*, **8**(3).

van Praag, B.M.S., Hagenaars, A.J.M. and van Weeren, H. (1982), 'Poverty in Europe', *Review of Income and Wealth*, **28**, 345–59.

Verma, V.K. (1996), *Longitudinal Response Rate: Empirical Results*, ECHP Pan 73/96, Colchester: University of Essex.

Walker, R. and Ashworth, K. (1994), *Poverty Dynamics: Issues and Examples*, Aldershot: Avebury.

Williams, F. and Pillinger, J. (1996), 'New thinking on social policy research into inequality, social exclusion and poverty', in J. Millar and J. Bradshaw (eds), *Social Welfare Systems: Towards a Research Agenda*, Bath Social Policy Papers, No. 24, University of Bath: Centre for the Analysis of Social Policy.

Index

Titles of publications are in *italics*.